D0396464

Jazz Heritage

Jazz Heritage

MARTIN WILLIAMS

New York   Oxford
OXFORD UNIVERSITY PRESS
1985

Oxford University Press

Oxford   London   New York   Toronto
Delhi   Bombay   Calcutta   Madras   Karachi
Kuala Lumpur   Singapore   Hong Kong   Tokyo
Nairobi   Dar es Salaam   Cape Town
Melbourne   Auckland

and associated companies in
Beirut   Berlin   Ibadan   Mexico City   Nicosia

Copyright © 1985 by Martin Williams
Published by Oxford University Press, Inc.,
200 Madison Avenue, New York, New York 10016

All rights reserved. No part of this publication may be reproduced, stored
in a retrieval system, or transmitted, in any form or by any means, elec-
tronic, mechanical, photocopying, recording, or otherwise, without the prior
permission of Oxford University Press.

Library of Congress Cataloging in Publication Data
Williams, Martin T.
  Jazz heritage.
  Includes index.
  1. Jazz music—Addresses, essays, lectures.
2. Jazz musicians.
I. Title.
ML3507.W53   1985   785.42   85-4815
ISBN 0-19-503611-5

Printing (last digit): 9 8 7 6 5 4 3 2 1
Printed in the United States of America

Acknowledgment is hereby made of permission to reprint in somewhat different form essays first published by the following:

American Music. A Quarterly Journal: What Happened in Kansas City?

Annual Review of Jazz Studies: Count Basie in the 1950s. By permission of *Annual Review of Jazz,* Rutgers, the State University of New Jersey.

Barnaby Records: The World of Cecil Taylor. Courtesy of Barnaby Records, Inc.

down beat: What Does a Jazz Composer Do?; Videotaping with Duke; Monk at Rehearsal; Thad and Mel at the Vanguard; and Cultural Diggings. By permission of *down beat* magazine.

Fantasy, Inc.: Honoring Bill Evans; The Immortal Jelly Roll Morton; The Immortal King Oliver; Miles Davis: Walkin'; Miles Davis and the Modern Jazz Giants; Thelonius Monk: The Golden Monk; Thelonius Monk: The High Priest; Sonny Rollins: Saxophone Colossus.

Grove Press: Third Stream Problems; Talking with Myself; Mulligan and Desmond in the Studio; and Homage à Hodeir.

Institute for Studies in American Music: Jazz, the Phonograph, and Scholarship. Reprinted from *The Phonograph and Our Musical Life,* ed. II. Wiley Hitchcock (Brooklyn, 1980).

Jazz Times: Just Asking.

Metronome: Rehearsing with Ornette. Robert Asen. Metronome Collection.

Music Educators Journal: What Does a Jazz Composer Do? Copyright © 1975 by Music Educators National Conference.

New World Records: Cuttin' the Boogie. This essay originally appeared as liner notes for New World NW 259 "Cuttin' the Boogie," © 1977 Recorded Anthology of American Music, Inc. All rights reserved.

Parker Records: Once There Was a Bird: Charlie Parker.

Saturday Review: The Rediscovery of Earl Hines, © 1965; In Praise of Jack Teagarden, © 1964; The Comic Mask of Fats Waller, © 1966; Guitar by Charlie Christian, © 1969; Ella and Her Critics, © 1966; In Memoriam, Bud Powell, © 1966; Albert Alyer, For Example, © 1965. All copyright by Saturday Review Magazine.

Stereo Review: Recording Miles Davis. Copyright © 1984. Ziff-Davis Publishing Company.

Teresa Gramophone: Classic Tenors: Coleman Hawkins and Lester Young.

for Mark, Rick, and Doug —friends

PREFACE

My book contains examples of every kind of short essay through which writers have approached jazz—every kind except straight interviews and short biographical sketches.

In the first section the reader will find both extended appreciations and shorter reviews. In these and in the other selections here, I have made some small revisions over the initial appearances of the pieces, and have not hesitated to second-guess myself here and there. But where more extended additional comment or discographical information seemed called for, I have made it in an added new paragraph or two which I have dated.

The second section of *Jazz Heritage* describes players and ensembles on the job, in recording studios, night clubs, TV studios—a more revealing form of observation, on occasion, than the more self-conscious interview.

In "Annotations" I have salvaged examples of writing from the sleeves of LP records, a form of comment which I think finds its way into book form less often than it should. I have made my choices there because of the artists discussed, the quality of the music recorded, or (in most cases) both.

In the final section, I have included some observations on jazz criticism and one jazz critic in particular. I have also addressed the somewhat peripheral question of the Afro-American contribution to our musical theater. And I have tried to take a hard look at some of the problems jazz has encountered since this once-scorned idiom has found its way to respectability, and its future appreciation has been turned over in part to our academics.

I hope that *Jazz Heritage* will seem a self-contained statement. In a sense, it may also be seen as a complement to my earlier book *The Jazz Tradition*. In the first section, I have included figures not discussed in that book, in later sections I have included still more of them and tried to observe such men as Duke Ellington, Miles Davis, Thelonious Monk, Ornette Coleman, and others from different perspectives.

I have made all my selections in the hope that a view of jazz and its musicians and singers from four somewhat different points of view will make us understand the music differently, and above all, help us hear it better.

Martin Williams

Alexandria, Virginia
March 1985

ॐ

ACKNOWLEDGMENTS

I began writing about jazz in my school paper (I must have been about sixteen) but my first real exposure came—it was about 1953—in the collectors magazine called *The Record Changer* with Bill Grauer as publisher and Orrin Keepnews as editor, both of them also founders of Riverside Records.

When Whitney Balliett ceased writing for the *Saturday Review* in 1957, to take up jazz for *The New Yorker,* he and Nat Hentoff recommended that I replace him to SR's Irving Kolodin. Kolodin agreed, and that gave me my first "professional" writing—that is, the first for which I was paid.

I was to try taking a different approach to the music than was common at the time, and the encouragement of Gunther Schuller then and subsequently has been of continuing importance.

Sheldon Meyer was editor of my first book, the anthology *The Art of Jazz,* in 1959 and he has seen me through four volumes since, two on jazz, and one each on movies, and on television.

Gratitude of the sort I owe these men does not go without saying, and it is a privilege these several decades later to offer it in print.

In preparing this volume, I have sought guidance from Gary Giddins, Rick Woodward, Mark Tucker, and Doug Richards. The contents here would not have been the same without them.

Following the copyright page of this book, the reader will find a sizable list of credits and copyrights covering the original sources and permissions for the pieces included herein. I am most grateful for them all, but here I would like to offer additional thanks to Paul Clark, Associate Publisher of *The Saturday Review;* Bob Thiele; Jack Maher of *Down Beat;* Elizabeth Ostrow of New World records; Paul Zaentz of Fantasy for the notes in the third section on Morton, Oliver, Davis, Monk, and Rollins as well as the Bill Evans essay; Robert Asen and the Metronome Collection; Barney Rossett of Grove Press; Ira Sabin of *Jazz Times;* and H. Wiley Hitchcock of the Institute for Studies in American Music of Brooklyn College C.U.N.Y.

M.W.

⪧

CONTENTS

I

Comments and Questions

ॐ

THE REDISCOVERY OF
EARL HINES

By 1928 Louis Armstrong had begun to attract musical associates equal to the task that he had outlined, that of revitalizing jazz and leading its players out of a declining New Orleans style and into what was to become its "swing" era. The most brilliant among those associates was pianist Earl Hines, and with him Armstrong recorded such small-group classics as *Muggles, West End Blues, Skip the Gutter,* and the trumpet-piano duet *Weather Bird.* At the same time, Hines was recording such solo classics of his own as *Blues in Thirds* and *I Ain't Got Nobody.*

The 1950s, however, found Earl Hines a member of a strident Dixieland "revival" band in San Francisco—an experience that might long since have embittered a lesser artist. And this relatively obscure musical life was punctuated only by a couple of bookings with a trio into the kind of after-theater clubs that feature self-effacing music, as an unobtrusive accompaniment to the patrons' conversation.

It is not enough to say that Earl Hines played in his fifties and his sixties as well as he once had, for it may be that he played better, and he certainly played with more creative energy and devotion to his idiom than such an immediate follower as Teddy Wilson does currently.

Hines's style has changed little since the twenties. There are momentary harmonic refinements perhaps in his essentially straightforward approach, and he no longer uses the brittle octaves in his right hand—an effort to be heard above the din of an earlier day. His left hand still walks smoothly in tenths, and still breaks them off briefly for complements

to his right or for forays into an *oom-pa* stride. His right
hand is still apt to enter the dazzling double-time rhythmic
mazes for which he is famous. Nowadays, if the dexterity of
his fingers may fail him momentarily, he still never loses
tempo or momentum. Hines also still knows how to use
dynamics teasingly and tellingly. And he still knows how to
paraphrase a theme and when to leave it to invent a new
one. But a renewed rhythmic vitality was what Hines
brought to the music, and the remarkable thing is that after
all these years his idiom is still fresh and moving when
played by the master.

Those of us who love jazz have come to accept a great
deal of carelessness and lassitude. We live with hours of
warming up, nights of creative enervation, weeks of coasting, months with young musicians thrust prematurely into
celebrity, and years with middle-aged men who infrequently
rise to the level of their illustrious younger days. What a
sublime pleasure it is to hear a man of Hines's years play so
rousingly, yet with such fine confidence and poise.

My evidence for the foregoing assertions comes, first, from
a series of appearances Hines made in March 1964 at the
Little Theater in New York, memorable concerts that were
everything that programs of semi-improvised music ought
to be, and, second, from a series of recent Hines LP releases.
"The Real Earl Hines" (Focus 335) was done on stage in the
final concert of the Little Theater series. It offers Hines's
charming spoken introduction, inviting the audience to an
informal evening of music. It contains a version of *Memories
of You,* a piece that obviously did not tempt Hines for its
quaintness but for its strength, and for the possibility of a
bit of mock melodrama. It has *I Ain't Got Nobody* in a performance still full of drive after thirty-six years in Hines's
hands. It has *Tea for Two,* a tired warhorse in which Hines
finds unexpectedly delicate melody, good parody, and com-

mendably timed changes of tempo. And it has an agonizing trill of several choruses on *St. Louis Blues,* a moment of winning showmanship to which Hines is fully entitled. The album's only drawback is that in the processing perhaps— the tape dubbing, the equalizing, and the rest—some of the vital "presence" of the music has been lost.

"Fatha," the New Earl Hines Trio (Columbia CL 2320; stereo CS 9120) offers Hines and the same otherwise sympathetic accompanists from the concert—Ahmed Abdul-Malik, bass, and Al Jackson, drums—but here they occasionally seem slightly out of phase with the leader. Hines comes on strong, sometimes as if he were after a hit (a redo of *Frankie and Johnny* boogie-woogie style, a bossa nova, and lots of tricky effects), and just weren't going to relax long enough to make his best music. However, there is an excellent reading of *Breezin' Along with the Breeze,* a very good one of *Broadway,* and there are fine choruses on *Believe It, Beloved* and *Louise.*

Spontaneous Explorations (Contact CN 2; stereo CS 2) offers Hines's piano unaccompanied (except for an occasionally audible light foot-tapping) and done, I understand, in an afternoon's work with a minimum of retakes. It is the most consistent and in many ways the best of the albums under review. It is certainly an utterly charming recital, with Hines's sometimes luxuriant and always crucial left hand beautifully audible throughout. There are splendid readings of *Undecided, I've Found a New Baby, Squeeze Me, Tosca's Dance* (a version of one of Hines's earliest pieces, actually), and a soundly showy *You Always Hurt the One You Love.* There is also a Tatum-esque *Jim* and a *Fatha's Blues,* an example of how much expressive introspection Hines, no down-home blues man, can find in the form. (*1965*)

Indeed, Hines made some of the best recordings of his

career after his 1964 re-emergence. The Contact album discussed above reappeared as half of a two-record set on Flying Dutchman FD 10147, *"The Mighty Fatha,"* and by the time this appears may have shown up on that label's successor label Doctor Jazz—or if it hasn't, it should have. *"Paris Session"* on Ducretet Thompson Dux 40262 is an outstanding collection of Hines interpretations of standards. And *"The Quintessential Earl Hines"* (Halcyon HAL 101) revisits the early Hines classics like *Blues in Thirds, My Monday Date, Panther Rag, Chimes in Blues,* etc., in extended versions to give us unique dual statements on the same material by a youthfully ebullient and a seasoned and mature jazz artist.

The earlier versions from the 1928 QRS label of the same material were collected on Milestone MLP 2012, and those from Okeh are included in the Smithsonian's *"Louis Armstrong and Earl Hines"* 1928 (#2002).

Finally, a great Hines event of 1984 (the year following his death): the appearance of a complete Little Theater concert on a two-record set on Muse MR 2001-2. I have reservations about the quality of the sound, but none of the reservations about the lack of presence in the performances that I expressed above. And, because of a slight harmonic disagreement between Hines and guest tenor saxophonist Bud Johnson at the beginning of *Lester Leaps In* (Hines goes for the blues rather than *I Got Rhythm* chords), I'd guess that this album is the *first* Little Theater concert complete. *(1984)*

ॐ

IN PRAISE OF
JACK TEAGARDEN

The audience might be composed of the sort of avid fans who would applaud no matter what he played. Or it might be only partly attentive. In either case he seemed to play and sing with complete relaxation and professional poise. Yet if you watched his quietly genial face closely, you might see a fleeting frown or a quick downward turn at the corners of his mouth that would let you know that he hadn't been quite satisfied with what he had just done, that the last solo hadn't come off as well as he had wanted it to.

Jack Teagarden (who died on January 15, 1965, in New Orleans) was a professional jazz musician for more than forty years, performing night after night in situations that were sometimes trying or downright harassing. And, by the nature of his craft, he had to extemporize at least some of his music each time he undertook to play it. Yet, on occasion, he remained capable of exacting self-criticism.

Teagarden was one of those exceptional musicians who, by the late twenties, perceived not only what jazz had achieved, but also which part of that achievement seemed most worth preserving and what such music might best undertake next. This means that Teagarden belongs with Louis Armstrong (who towers above the rest), with Bix Beiderbecke, with Earl Hines, with Coleman Hawkins, in the advance guard of the period. (Sidney Bechet belongs with them, too, yet Bechet, as Ernest Ansermet pointed out at the time, was already a major figure by 1919.) All these men were very good instrumentalists; each in his way knew his instrument as many of his important predecessors in jazz had not known theirs. And Teagarden was a superb trombonist by almost any standard. Teagarden shares with Jimmy Harrison, and a handful of their immediate followers, the distinction of having lifted the trombone from its mournfully effective, sometimes clownish percussive-harmonic role at the bottom of the Dixieland ensemble and raised it to the level of a subtle, flexible melodic voice in jazz. Yet each of these men, certainly Teagarden and Harrison themselves, initially found his way for himself, independently of the others.

Weldon Leo Teagarden was born in Vernon, Texas, in 1905. His parents were both of German ancestry (and apparently not with any American Indian ancestry as is sometimes said), and both were musical. So were and are their other children: trumpeter Charlie, drummer Clois, and pianist Norma. Jack began piano at five; then he had some lessons on the baritone horn; and finally his father presented him with a trombone. He was playing professional jobs by 1920, when his family was living in Oklahoma City, and he was already developing the largely self-discovered trombone technique that he retained all his life. He spent the early twenties barnstorming through Oklahoma, New Mexico, Texas, and northern Mexico with various dance groups, moving as far away as Kansas City in 1924.

Three years later he was in New York. The word was out among jazzmen about his abilities. He continued of necessity to work with the sort of semicommercial orchestras that were to earn him his bread and butter until the late thirties—groups like Sam Lanin's and Roger Wolfe Kahn's. With drummer Ben Pollack's orchestra, Teagarden, Benny Goodman, and Jimmy McPartland could often share a final chorus or two of jazz, improvising after a grim opening ensemble and sometimes a quaint "period" vocal chorus. Meanwhile, Teagarden was making his most important early recordings with various casual "pickup" combinations under various leaderships. He remained in commercial dance groups (Mal Hallett's and Paul Whiteman's) until late 1938 when he formed his own big band, which continually struggled with financial unsuccess until 1947. Then he joined Louis Armstrong's newly formed small group, staying with him until 1951. Teagarden led a small quasi-Dixieland group of his own.

If I seem to be making a historical figure of Jack Teagarden by my claims to his role in the twenties, it is very far from my intention. He left a large and uneven heritage of recordings, but the unevenness is not always his fault.

Teagarden was capable of creating and sustaining a very special, personal aura, even in adverse circumstances—even in the company of a man like Louis Armstrong, whose grandiloquent statements are emotionally quite removed from Teagarden's deceptively easy, self-contained moments. There was, for example, a superb evening in 1947 at New York's Town Hall with Armstrong and Teagarden that virtually renewed the careers of both men and happily was recorded.

Teagarden was able to follow Armstrong's devastating vocal burlesque on one of his specialties, *Pennies from Heaven,* with a half-chorus solo that is an effortless lyric gem. He makes very little of the melody line of that piece as written; he invents one of his own that is more interesting and is punctuated by typical Teagarden virtuoso flourishes. Some of those flourishes come close to decorativeness, and they have a kind of quiet elegance that one would never hear from an Armstrong. Yet nothing in that half-chorus seems *merely* decorative, and that, I think, is a good measure of his talent.

On the same stage and the same evening Teagarden did *St. James Infirmary.* In it we have the best example I know of the Teagarden aura, the calm, almost lazy, deceptively understated, musical demeanor that is all firmness and power under the surface.

Like Armstrong or Billie Holiday—for that matter, like Leopold Stokowski—Teagarden returned to the same repertory year after year. He could do *Beale Street Blues, After You've Gone, Stars Fell on Alabama, Sheik of Araby, Basin Street Blues,* and the rest night after night; do them well; and occasionally do them as if this night were going to be the last. And he could also do them very differently. There is another good *St. James Infirmary* from 1940, with Teagarden and the then-Ellingtonians (Rex Stewart, Barney Bigard, and Ben Webster) that not only offers different musical ideas but a radically different emotional approach to the piece.

I have said that in *Pennies from Heaven* Teagarden's solo is largely an invention. So also is his early, celebrated *Sheik of Araby* from 1930 with Red Nichols, wherein Teagarden invented out of the chords while a lesser trombonist, Glenn Miller, hummed the original theme behind him.

However, most of Teagarden's best solos are paraphrases of melodies as written, and they show his taste in knowing what to add, what to leave out, what to rephrase. I have a particular favorite, the 1956 version of *My Kinda Love.* The piece has a very good main melody, but the "bridge" or "middle" part of the song is not so good, except that it has a charming final descending phrase. On the recording, Teagarden has his solo on that bridge, and he wisely keeps that final phrase. However, he tosses out the inferior beginning, inventing a new one. It is a good one, which also leads up to that final phrase more logically and beautifully.

On *After You've Gone,* also from 1956, the trombonist alternates the written phrases from that familiar piece with inventions of his own. If one refuses to care about how the original is supposed to go, Teagarden's version does not fall into disparate pieces, but has a clear and original logic of its own.

Although it seems spurious to me to describe Teagarden as "the king" of blues trombonists, as recent album huckstering does, I am sure that (unlike Hines and Beiderbecke, for examples) he was authentically a blues man, that he could play the twelve-bar blues with a real feel for the idiom, and not just play in the form. And I am also sure that, like many another important jazzman, he could use such blues feeling discreetly no matter what sort of piece he was playing. His blues playing was not like any other man's blues. That, it seems to me, attests to the individuality Teagarden was able to find in the idiom, not to a lack of authenticity.

The indigenous twelve-bar form is surely the core of the Teagarden heritage on record. He did *Makin' Friends* vocally and instrumentally on his first important record date in 1928 with an Eddie Condon ensemble. And Teagarden's preliminary solo on the 1929 *Knockin' a Jug* survives even after Louis Armstrong's final bravura statement at the end of the record. Following these, there were the variants of *Makin' Friends* like *Dirty Dog, That's a Serious Thing* (which, incidentally, forecast Harold Arlen's *Stormy Weather* melody), *Jack Hits the Road,* etc., which punctuate his subsequent career in the studios. An exceptional tribute occurs on *The Blues* from a 1939 *Metronome* magazine-poll "all star" recording: Tommy Dorsey refused to solo as long as Teagarden was present, but finally played a discreet background to Teagarden's blues improvising.

The strength in his blues playing also provides an answer to those who have said that a sentimentality in his work accounts for his durability as a popular performer. It also seems to me that any committed sentimentality in a man who performed *Stars Fell on Alabama* night after night would have done him in long ago. I doubt if a sentimentalist could have gotten through the elaborate Teagarden introductions and codas without playing the fool. I have mentioned elegance and his penchant for flourishes, but elegance is not weakness and flourishes are not frou-frou.

An ability to play a simple blues well is a good esthetic test for a man who can obviously perform on more sophisticated melodies and harmonies. Similarly, an ability to rediscover the early jazz repertory and return to the simpler structures of *Muskrat Ramble* or *Panama* or *My Monday Date* is also a test, and Teagarden did all these pieces well with the Armstrong All Stars.

It has been said that Teagarden's voice is almost a version of his trombone; like many other voices, it deepened through the years, and thereby it became even more like his trombone. Conversely, we can hear how much of his flexibility on trombone simply had to be self-taught because it is so personally vocalized. (This also applies to his device of removing the bell of his horn and muting the end of its tubing with a water glass, the only trombone mute he ever cared to use.) He recorded trombone and vocal versions of *Basin Street Blues* many times but a comparison of two of the best versions, from 1931 with Benny Goodman and 1956 with Bobby Hackett, is fine evidence of his durability.

Teagarden had a genuine desire to reach people with his music, but that desire had nothing to do with compromise. He was always well-mannered; he would show you musically how he felt without apology, but he would never accost you musically and demand that you be moved. And he was unapologetically himself and true to his talent. Thereby, Jack Teagarden walked with an artistic dignity all his life. (*1964*)

To say that Jack Teagarden did what he set out to do superbly is not to deny that he remained stylistically under

Louis Armstrong's spell until the end. Dickie Wells, out-standingly among the important immediate successors of Teagarden and Jimmy Harrison, made something more personal from what he got from Armstrong. And so, each in his way, did Benny Morton, J. C. Higgenbotham, Vic Dickerson, and others.

Teagarden's "cool Louis" remains nevertheless distinctive—and of course he remains, technically, an exceptional trombonist. Indeed, the 1950 version of *Lover* which, he recorded on the Jump label under Charlie La Vere's name, for all its occasional rhythmic stiffness, floored the beboppers of the time for its technical and inventive prowess—and still impresses all brass players, as well as the rest of us.

And, by the way, the complete Louis Armstrong 1947 Town Hall Concert, with Teagarden's *St. James Infirmary* and his *Pennies from Heaven* solo has now appeared on a French RCA two-record set PM 45374. One's conclusion is that the high praise which that evening received at the time was fully deserved. And that Armstrong's return to small-group music was as auspicious as we have long been told that it was.

For the ardent record collector, I can be of only limited further encouragement, for as this is written I find none of the Teagarden titles I have mentioned available on domestic labels. However, the French are responsible for the complete Armstrong Town Hall Concert set, so the best advice would (again) be to ransack well-stocked dealers' import bins and see what the French, British, Italians, Japanese, and Germans may be doing for the Teagarden classics. (*1984*)

ॐॐ

THE COMIC MASK OF
FATS WALLER

Thomas "Fats" Waller was a pianist, singer, and songwriter, but his first love was the organ. He would play the instrument whenever he could, alone and deeply absorbed, for hours at a time, performing all kinds of music on it and particularly Bach. "But," he would remark, "who wants a colored organist?"

The answer is that a few hundred ambitiously middle-class Negro churches around the country would have wanted one—such churches as undertake baroque chorales rather than gospel songs—these churches would have wanted one, provided the organist were content to live in modest obscurity. But obscurity was not for Fats Waller; both by destiny and by choice, success and fame were. In gaining that fame, Waller paid a price that involved not only sacrificing the organ but sacrificing perhaps half of his talent.

To be sure, the successful Fats is pretty nearly irresistible. This is the Waller who entered a recording studio with his "Rhythm" (usually a sextet), to be handed some inane current ditty and who proceeded to record it with frequently hilarious vocal parody and general good musical spirits. We are reminded of this Fats again and again on RCA Victor's new Vintage reissue of sixteen Waller numbers (LPV-525), most of them recorded during 1935 and 1936, and on the Waller Vintage release of a few months back (LPV-517).

Waller's pseudo-operatic histrionics in undertaking a Bobby Breen specialty called *Let's Sing Again* are side-splitting. His mock misery in reheating the *Sugar Blues* did the sort of permanent damage to subsequent performances of that piece that the Marx Brothers did to *Il Trovatore*.

The effect of Waller's vocal mugging is immediate, winning, complete—and it all sounds easy. It *was* easy, I think, and, for most of the musical aspects of Waller's talent, it was also limiting. Only a complex man could have held experience at arm's length by means of such good comedy, to be sure, but a complex and musically gifted man like Waller might have done a lot more.

Waller was so good a composer that, given a chance to record some piano originals, he might walk into the studio virtually unprepared and simply knock off a couple of pieces. They would be respectable and probably good—or good enough. Of course, if Fats Waller were not capable of excellence, it wouldn't matter too much. But Waller was capable of excellence, and he showed it often enough to make the totality of his musical output a joy, a frustration, and finally a tragedy.

A respected younger musician wondered recently if any of Waller's music could be said to survive. I confess I was shocked that he would even pose such a question. In the first place, the bursting joy with which Waller's piano could interpret a line like *Why Do I Lie to Myself About You?* or the pensiveness he brought to *Thief in the Night,* or his technical jubilance on *I Got Rhythm* are enough to make one want to hear him.

Second, Waller wrote at least three superb and somewhat neglected melodies: *Squeeze Me, Black and Blue,* and *Honeysuckle Rose* (and incidentally, himself recorded only the last in an adequate version). These to me are the great Waller compositions, not just the post-ragtime piano pieces, of which we have examples in *Valentine Stomp* and *Goin' About* on the Vintage releases.

Then there is Waller's sense of structure as an improviser, a quality in which his predecessors and teachers like James P. Johnson and Willie "the Lion" Smith gave him good lessons. There is a fine example of this in the Vintage series in the blues he called *Numb Fumblin'*; he alternates robust percussive choruses with highly lyric episodes back and forth, building each in complexity, until the two moods come together in choruses of shimmering virtuosity at the end.

Personally, I am still waiting for the LP appearance of several of Waller's best solo recordings, including his superb variations on *Keepin' Out of Mischief Now,* his pensive reading of *Georgia on My Mind,* his *Tea for Two,* and his solo version of *Honeysuckle Rose.*

Waller did burlesque and cajole the poor tunes he was handed to record, but it was not often given to him to work a change by spontaneously rewriting such ditties as Billie Holiday did. Nor was it given to him to fuse together his penchant for humor and his musicality, as a successor like Thelonious Monk has done. On occasion Waller did use his talents as a clown to hold his audience while he also offered them the gifted and reflective musician who lay under the surface, but, alas, all too infrequently.

If Waller had managed against odds that were admittedly great, to bring together all the elements within him—the fine pianist, the irresistible clown, the exceptional composer, the introspective after-hours organist—he would, I think, belong with that handful of geniuses that jazz has so far produced.

As it is, he does belong in a place of his own, very carefully labeled "Thomas 'Fats' Waller." And in that place Waller the clown shines in spite of everything we say. His antics on *Somebody Stole My Gal, Dust Off That Old Pianna,* and *If This Isn't Love* might almost be taken as definitive of Negro American humor and its attitudes. And those attitudes include a penetrating and unexpected parody of the kind of "shiftless darky" humor that white America has expected of blacks. Such comedy, done as well as Fats Waller did it, has its place in the scheme of things—as the gods surely will agree. (*1966*)

Neither of the Vintage albums mentioned above was long in print, but a subsequent RCA reissue program, reviving the old Bluebird label logo, undertook a "complete" Waller in a series of albums. In view of the reverence expressed above for Waller the soloist, there should be no doubt that I looked forward to the entry in that series that collected Waller's solo piano recordings, *A Handful of Keys* through *I Ain't Got Nobody,* with all the titles cited above as well. Alas, the transfers for that album proved to be full of tape flutter and *wow,* and they produced pitches that wavered shockingly.

Meanwhile there had been a French RCA collected Waller, good transfers but available, as of this writing, only as a boxed set—a situation (one hopes) subject to change. (*1984*)

ß❧

WHAT HAPPENED IN KANSAS CITY?

It is generally agreed that in the decades of the 1920s and the 1930s there were important developments in jazz which centered in Kansas City. Kansas City had been the home of the Bennie Moten orchestra since the early 1920s, it gave us the Count Basie orchestra with Lester Young in the mid-1930s, and it nurtured Charlie Parker before he came to national prominence in the 1940s. Such a city, such a musical environment, obviously warrants attention, and so far it has been given not nearly enough.

Among the reliable sources, there is a highly provocative interlude in *Hear Me Talkin' to Ya* (1955), a collection of excerpts from interviews edited by Nat Shapiro and Nat Hentoff, "From Kansas City, a Musician's town. . . ." That section offers then-new quotations from pianist-composer Mary Lou Williams, pianist Sammy Price, drummer Jo Jones, and excerpts from earlier interviews with other participants. The pioneering effort at a history is Frank Driggs's chapter "Kansas City and the Southwest" in *Jazz* (1959), edited by Hentoff and Albert McCarthy, a chapter which Driggs is scheduled to expand into a book which we can look forward to.

For musical analysis and criticism there is Gunther Schuller's perceptive, detailed examination of the surviving recordings from the beginnings to the early 1930s, "The Southwest," in *Early Jazz* (1968).

Unpublished and virtually unknown are the oral history tapes done in the 1970s by Nathan Pearson and Howard Litwack, copies of which reside in the Kansas City Museum and at the Institute of Jazz Studies at Rutgers University in Newark, New Jersey.

What I would like to offer is an interpretation of Kansas City's musical history through 1940, one which will benefit from Driggs's work and from Schuller's. Kansas City, an "open" city, under the control of the notorious political "machine" of Tom Prendergast: there were large ballrooms and there were less pretentious dance halls; there were cabarets, clubs; there was gambling; there was prostitution. There was a constant call for music, and like New Orleans

before it, Kansas City offered welcoming gestures to the remarkable Afro-American improvisational music called jazz.

We can best establish the nature of some of the best of
that music with recordings by the Bennie Moten orchestra.
But we might start, not with one of the earliest Motens but
with some of the last and most important.

The spirited *Moten Swing* is a set of instrumental variations, written and improvised, on a popular song of the
time by Walter Donaldson, *You're Driving me Crazy. Toby*
is a series of written and improvised variations on the standard American popular song, Victor Young's *Sweet Sue
(Just You)*. We have an ensemble of three trumpets, two
trombones, three saxophones, piano, guitar, bass, and drums,
and featuring among others Oran "Hot Lips" Page as trumpet soloist; Eddie Durham tripling as trombonist, occasional
solo guitarist, and occasional composer-arranger; Ben Webster on tenor saxophone; and Bill (later Count) Basie on
piano. The remarkable final riffs on *Toby* were the work of
the band's saxophonist-clarinetist Eddie Barefield (with one
borrowing from Gene Gifford's *Casa Loma Stomp*).

Those two recordings, and at least four others made on
the same occasion (*Blue Room, Milenberg Joys, Lafayette,*
and *Prince of Wales*), are exceptionally spirited, well played,
and in a style several years ahead of their time. But when
one learns the circumstances under which they were played,
they become even more worthy of our respect. They were
recorded at the end of a disastrous Depression-era Eastern
tour for a Moten orchestra that was already losing its following. The musicians found their way to Victor's Camden,
New Jersey, studios literally hungry; they dined on one
stewed rabbit provided by a helpful fan; and the following
morning they recorded.

Notice again what they recorded. We are speaking here
of a music which must find its own audience and which

must compete for that audience with musics of all kinds. What does one do when times are hard, when one's career is on the skids, when one is losing his audience? Obviously, he re-records his old hits, or he does "cover" versions of other people's hits, or he tries to come up with new material in the old style to please his surviving audience. But these men did none of those things. Under the most adverse circumstances, and like all good jazz musicians, they set down the best and most advanced music they knew how to make.

A Bennie Moten ensemble had been around since the early 1920s. And by 1924, on its third record date and with its personnel expanded from six to eight, it had its first hit in a piece called *South*. Indeed, a 1928 stylistically updated Moten re-make of *South* with ten instrumentalists, two trumpets, a trombone, three reeds, and four rhythm, could be found in jukeboxes in the South and Southwest well into the 1940s.

The debt of the first version of *South* to the New Orleans style is obvious, specifically to the first recorded version of that style by the Original Dixieland Jazz Band. And it seems to me that, like that group, the early Moten records capture the raucous irreverence of the style but little of the deeper passion, joy, and shared humanity we encounter on the best recordings of King Oliver or Jelly Roll Morton.

However, from those beginnings, the Moten band grew and flourished, and around its success and its prominence Kansas City jazz grew and flourished for nearly two decades.

Indeed, it spread. By the late 1920s, the second most successful ensemble in town was led by George E. Lee, and George Lee's staff composer was Jesse Stone. Stone had had his own ensemble in St. Louis, and by April 1927 that group had recorded a still-celebrated brass passage on a piece called *Starvation Blues*.

In general, I think what we hear in Kansas City jazz in the 1920s is a disciplined dance music whose strengths lie in its energy, its ensemble verve—in that fine paradox of power and relaxation that we hear in so much jazz—and in the skill and insight with which its composer manipulated in the common musical coin of the period. We have little reason to believe there were any great improvisers among the soloists. Many of the solos, even some of the strongest, were apparently written out. Also, the trumpeters in some of Moten's early records seem clearly indebted to Bix Beiderbecke or Red Nichols, long after the best players in the East were following in Louis Armstrong's footsteps.

In such a context, what made *Moten Swing* possible in 1932? The answer lies in the earlier ensemble of bass-player Walter Page and its personnel. Page led a gathering of ambitious young musicians called Blue Devils between 1926 and 1931. The Blue Devils had developing soloists, particularly in "Hot Lips" Page, William Basie, Eddie Durham, and singer Jimmy Rushing. Moten began to hire away such players from Page one by one, and by 1932 he had almost all of them plus tenor saxophonist Ben Webster. Meanwhile, Page had made his single, two-sided recording in 1929. One of the two selections, *There's a Squabblin'*, has a fine and prominent use of ensemble riff figures and it gives us some idea of what Moten had been acquiring.

We have recorded evidence of what the Moten band sounded like as it was acquiring Page's musicians but had not yet acquired Page. From late 1929, there is *Jones Law Blues*,* credited to Basie and Moten, with two trumpets, two trombones, three saxophones, and four rhythm including tuba, and Durham and Basie both present.

Details aside, the *Jones Law Blues* shows no important

---

* The "Jones" statute forbade any establishment to advertise that it served or sold liquor, an apparent effort to stave off the prohibitionists.

changes in the Moten style. Nor in any style, for that matter, for the performance may remind us of one of Jelly Roll Morton's late Victor records, and those are hardly Morton's most celebrated recordings. But the fact that Page himself is not present, and not present on string bass, makes a crucial difference.

What was needed so that an ensemble could *swing*, could play with the new Louis Armstrong-inspired momentum—the "triplet feel" of Armstrong's melodic rhythm—was what Schuller has called "the democratization of the beats." That is, that all four beats in a 4/4 measure be of equal emphasis and equal value. The musicians realized that to follow Armstrong's lead, the pulse had to change, and a wind bass simply could not execute four-to-a-bar at any but the slowest tempos.

The Moten band was not unique in 1932 in being able to swing as an ensemble. Indeed, an Armstrong-inspired swing on the part of the individual young soloists can be heard beginning in 1924 and 1925. For the next eight years, the quality was gradually absorbed by jazz composers and arrangers and by the full ensembles, and by 1932 jazz orchestras—including the best of them like Fletcher Henderson's and Duke Ellington's—had either learned to swing collectively or they were destined to pass out of existence.

Moten Swing, Toby, and the rest were the beginning of the end for the Moten band, however. The group found its way back to Kansas City, and whatever hopes its members had that the new records would mean new work went unfulfilled. The year 1935 found Basie leading the remnants of Moten's ensemble, nine men, in a little club called the Reno. The music was informal, to say the least, the "book"—the music, the arrangements—carried largely in the players' heads, and the performances largely depended on the im-

provising prowess of the players, plus the verve with which
it could play occasional ensemble effects. Informal or not,
Basie's group soon gained its own kind of polish. As Basie
has put it, ". . . we worked together a long while. We got
so we coordinated every move, every solo, perfectly."

Basie's Reno Club group included Ed Lewis and "Lips"
Page (later Buck Clayton) on trumpets; Buster Smith (later
Jack Washington) and Lester Young on saxophones; Dan
Minor on trombone; Jo Jones on drums, plus Basie and
Walter Page. And it seems to me evident that the style they
offered was based on bringing the Kansas City jam session—
or a modified version of it—out in public and onto the
bandstand.

The Kansas City jam session was a fabled institution.
Pianist Sammy Price, up from Honey Grove, Texas, put it
this way:

> Jam sessions in Kansas City? I remember once at the Sub-
> way Club, on Eighteenth Street, I came by a session at
> about ten o'clock and then went home to clean up and
> change my clothes. I came back a little after one o'clock
> and they were still playing the same song.

Such occasions are sometimes misunderstood. The Kansas
City jam sessions were not simply competitive "cutting con-
tests," combats through which a trumpeter or saxophonist
could challenge the champion. Nor were they only occasions
when big band sidemen could improvise without restraint.
They were educational institutions; they were the informal
conservatories of these musicians. As Jo Jones has explained:

> There were jam sessions I used to watch there and other
> places in Kansas City, even before I got with the Basie
> band, that were unlike any other jam sessions I have heard

since. It has to do with what I will try to explain to you about head arrangements in the Basie band and how we didn't have to rehearse back in Kansas City. It was just there and we played it.

Now it was a very strange thing at these jam sessions in Kansas City. Nobody ever got in nobody's way. Nobody ever had to point a finger and say: "You take it now. You take the next chorus." Any place in Kansas City where there was a session the guys would just get up on the bandstand, and spiritually they knew when to come in. They could tell when a guy had played his three or four choruses and was ready for someone else to take over. Like when there were either two tenors and two trumpet players on the stand no one had to point to you and tell you to follow the trombone player. They just felt which one was coming next.

There is no commercially recorded evidence of the nights at the Reno Club. There were broadcasts and I believe—or perhaps I only hope—that off-the-air recordings somewhere exist. In any case, we can gain *some* idea of what the Basie ensemble must have sounded like because in late 1936, a pseudonymous "Jones-Smith Incorporated" made four selections for Vocalion records. It was actually Basie and four of his men, plus trumpeter Carl Smith, playing music undoubtedly like what had been heard at the Reno.

Shoe Shine Boy from the Jones-Smith recordings is probably quite reliable evidence of the experimental freedom that these men evidently had at the club.* An ensemble with no written music, functioning in the commercial atmosphere of a nightclub, an ensemble that had to pay its way,

* I cite the originally released "take" of *Shoe Shine Boy* on which Basie's opening phrases show some quite uncharacteristic fumbling. An alternate, second take which has recently been released on LP has Basie playing cleanly. Young's solo work, while enlighteningly different, does not seem quite as good.

yet was able to make up not only its "book" but also its style, and to improvise its substance, in the most advanced manner its players desired.

There is little or nothing in the formal training of any of us, nothing in the way we have been taught to describe or think about music or any of the arts, that would lead us to think of such efforts as truly experimental. We are apt to think of *avant garde* music as made by unrecognized artists who are philanthropically subsidized. But I wonder if any American musician in the years 1935-36 had better support to be experimental, and successfully experimental, than these men at the Reno Club in Kansas City. In any case, they made an important music of a quality previously unheard.

Inevitably perhaps, but especially in view of its broadcasts, the Basie ensemble gradually attracted the attention of the powers in the music business and the record business. And Basie was encouraged to expand the group to the "big band" format of the time—three trumpets, two trombones, four saxophones, four rhythm. Basie accepted the idea willingly because he wanted a big band, but he wanted his big band "to work together just like those nine pieces did."

Count Basie and his orchestra had a first record date for Decca in January of 1937, and one of the four pieces it recorded was called *Roseland Shuffle*. *Roseland Shuffle* is another set of improvised variations on *Shoe Shine Boy* delivered for the most part in the then-unusual form of alternating, improvised four-bar phrases, "fours" in jazz parlance, by Basie and Lester Young. The performance is introduced by antiphonal brass-and-reeds; and climaxed by a chorus of brass and saxophone riffs.

Count Basie and his eight men made music in the Reno Club by putting the best aspects of the Kansas City "back room" session directly before its audience. And Count Basie preserved the integrity of that music when he increased the size of his group: he kept the ensemble effects functional and the solo work dominant. As Basie became a success, he needed to hire composer-arrangers to provide new music, and Basie became one of the great practical editors of other men's scores, always keeping the ensemble effects in their place and the performances open for his soloists.

This is not the place to retell the often-told story of the fresh qualities of the 1936 Basie band, its innovative rhythm section, and the work of its soloists. But I should offer a further word on Walter Page. He may not have been careful about the right note and the right chord, but he did provide the "solid four" beats I have described. And he took the rhythmic *lead* unto his instrument and away from the drums, a crucial step for the rhythm section.

Also, having included *Shoe Shine Boy* in the discussion, I will simply assert that Lester Young was the most original jazz improviser after Louis Armstrong, and draw attention to his opening phrases on that recording, where his usual high-handedness in handling a chord progression led to a rather complex chromatic juxtaposition.

Between instrumental blues like *One O'Clock Jump,* and vocal-instrumental blues like *Sent For You Yesterday,* most of the latter sung by Jimmy Rushing, perhaps 40 percent of Basie's music in the 1930s and 1940s was in twelve-bar blues form. And one might say that the Basie musicians were in effect playing the spirited Southwest blues, whatever the chord progression or whatever the phrase structure of the piece. Indeed, the spirit of the blues informs most of what came out of Kansas City in the 1930s. And the fact of the blues informed one of the most engaging musical duos of the period, the team of singer and ex-bartender Joe Turner and boogie woogie pianist (and ex-bouncer) Pete Johnson.

The national and international success of Count Basie inevitably led bookers, managers, and record producers to Kansas City in search of similar talent. "Lips" Page had already begun a career on his own; Johnson and Turner were recorded and brought to New York; Andy Kirk was rediscovered and began to record again; and saxophonist Harlan Leonard (who had helped Moten expand to eight pieces in the mid-1920s) led some big band records for the Bluebird label.

The next major event did not come to light nationally until 1941, however. When Basie moved to Columbia Records, Decca signed the group of pianist Jay McShann, and McShann's band, again like all good jazz ensembles, was interested in the growth and perfection of its idiom. Decca wanted more Basie-style blues, however, and it got them, but it also got a few more adventurous pieces, and it got the solos of an alto saxophonist named Charlie Parker who was soon to be recognized as the innovative improviser on whose work the "modernist" movement of the 1940s and 1950s was founded.

For Decca, Parker played outstanding solos on McShann's *Hootie Blues* and *The Jumpin' Blues* and on the AABA song-form piece *Sepian Bounce*. But more recently we have learned that Parker and McShann did not make their first records for the Decca company but made them privately for a citizen-fan in Wichita in November and December of 1940. These records recently found LP release and one of the pieces they include is a version of the venerable *Moten Swing* with a solo by Charlie Parker. The basic elements of his style can be heard—the developing speed and technique, the relative care with which he handled a chord progression, the linear inventiveness, and (above all) the already striking rhythmic originality of his phrase.

This too happened in Kansas City.

Recordings

The most recent domestic USA releases of the recordings mentioned in the text, including Moten's *Moten Swing, Toby,* and *Jones Law Blues* were on RCA Vintage LPV-514. *Starvation Blues* by George E. Lee is included in New World 256, as is the Walter Page Blue Devils' *There's a Squabblin'.*

Columbia CG 33502, "*The Lester Young Story, Volume 1,*" offers both takes of *Shoe Shine Boy.* And MCA 4050E has *Roseland Shuffle.*

Roll 'Em, Pete was last on Columbia KC 32708. The Mc-Shann Decca sessions, with *Hootie Blues, The Jumpin' Blues,* and *Sepian Bounce,* were on Decca DL 9236. And Onyx 221 has the McShann Wichita sessions with Charlie Parker on *Moten Swing.*

ঽ❧

COUNT BASIE IN THE 1950s
Horses in Midstream

Little has been written about the Count Basie orchestra of the 1950s and 1960s. Yet during that period there was a singular transformation of one of our most venerable musical institutions, a transformation and a renewed musical life. And the result was that an ensemble leader who had already made one major contribution to our music made another.

I say that "little" has been written, but by that I do not mean that nothing has been written. There is André Hodeir's essay "Basie's Way" in *Toward Jazz,* and there are Hsio Wen Shih's comments in his profile on Basie which largely echo Hodeir's view. And Hodeir's view seems to me largely wrongheaded. Yet, as with his essays on Art Tatum, Hodeir remains a true critic in that one cannot deal with his position without arriving solidly at one's own.

The Basie of the period can best be introduced by example. In 1959, the ensemble recorded an arrangement by Frank Foster of Duke Ellington's *In a Mellotone.* The piece is of course a casual, riff variation on the chord progression of Art Hickman's sentimental ballad *Rose Room (In Sunny Roseland),* and a minor Ellington masterpiece despite its relative informality and solo-oriented simplicity. It is ironic, therefore, that unusually casual Ellington should have been transformed into relatively formal Basie, but its very formality indicates the kind of transformation of Basie's music that came about in the 1950s.

If *In a Mellotone* is typical, then obviously this Basie orchestra is an ensemble whose virtues center on discipline, precision, and collective power. And in those respects, *In a Mellotone is* typical. It is also surprising, and placed in juxtaposition with music from Basie's early career, it becomes even more surprising.

Basie's attitude toward his music is well expressed in his response to a reporter's "What is your music about?" Basie paused, then said quietly, "Pat your foot." I expect that if his thinking were any less modest or any more pretentious, Basie could not accomplish for us what he has accomplished night after night, year after year. Basie knows far more than "pat your foot," to be sure; he would have to. But he also knows, I expect, that getting us to pat a foot is for his music the best basis from which to reach the rest of us.

The eight-piece Basie group which held forth at the Reno Club in Kansas City in 1935 had no formal "book" but only a collection of riffs and ensemble figures and chord progressions—largely borrowed, as we shall see—carried in the players' heads. And lots of improvised solos. The whole thing amounted to Basie's bringing some of the best elements of the informal Kansas City backroom jam session onto the bandstand before the public.

Let's dwell on some of the Basie borrowings. Buster Smith, the early group's lead saxophonist, has said of the best-known saxophone riff on *One O'Clock Jump* that Basie had simply called out to him to "set a riff" one night when the group was playing the blues in D-flat, and Smith had started to play a casually remembered paraphrase of Fats Waller's introduction to his *Six or Seven Times*.

There are many more examples from the early Basie book of such borrowings. Consider the opening riff to one of the 1938 successes, *Jumpin' at the Woodside*. It comes from *Jammin' for the Jackpot* from 1937 by the Mills Blue Rhythm Band, with composer credit to Eli Robinson, and can also be heard on *I Gotta Swing*, a 1935 recording by Blanche Calloway's band (composer credit not known, but Robinson was a member). And *Barrelhouse*, also by the Blue Rhythm Band, from 1936, with composer credit to Tab Smith, is clearly the source of Basie's 1939 *Jive at Five*, composer credit to Harry Edison.

The style of the Mills Blue Rhythm Band was not original. It was derived from Fletcher Henderson's, as were the styles of most of the big bands of the period, and its elements are easily described: antiphonal textures based on a separate, almost compartmentalized treatment of the saxophones (four in Basie's 1937 orchestra) vs. trumpets (four) vs. trombones (three), with the latter two sections only occasionally combined as a single brass voice, and a continuous harmonic-rhythmic accompaniment (from piano, guitar, string bass, and drums). Henderson also proved to be a major source of the early Basie book. For example, the closing brass riff of the 1932 Henderson arrangement of Fats Waller's *Honeysuckle Rose* was accompanied by a saxophone figure suggesting a "long meter" treatment of the melody line of Vincent Youmans's *Tea for Two*. Basie's 1937 arrangement used the same device. And Henderson's 1931 *Hot and Anxious* was the origin of Basie's 1938 *Swinging the Blues*.

I do not cite these examples to accuse Basie of leading a derivative ensemble. In the first place, everyone borrowed, even Ellington on occasion. Like all composers, these composers found their sources and their inspiration in whatever attracted them which they thought they could learn from and use. Albert Murray, Basie's collaborator in his autobiography, has put it that musicians place ideas in the public domain by playing them. In the second place, listening to the preceding examples juxtaposed can only bring out the informality and the very different spirit with which the Basie musicians interpreted this material, and the very different "feel" of the Basie rhythm section.

The borrowings become still less significant when we remember how they functioned. For Basie, the piece, the arrangement, was never the substance of the music. The substance was provided by the improvising soloists, as I have said. The arrangement—the score—was always the function of the interpreter's and the improviser's art.

The big swing bands flourished roughly from the mid-1930s through the late 1940s, and by the early 1950s there were only a handful of survivors. Since we Americans are very fond of interpreting events in our national life in terms of economics, we are apt to say that the bands disappeared because "the business" could no longer support them. But that is of course only another way of saying that large numbers of people no longer wanted to dance to their

music, listen to their music, or buy their recordings. However, I think there was a valid artistic reason why the bands
should not have survived. By the end of the 1940s their work
was largely done—almost all their ideas had been thoroughly
explored, thoroughly imitated and popularized, and only
the greatest or most individual of them—Ellington being
the supreme example—had pressing reasons to survive. The
Basie orchestra's artistic success had depended on its spirit,
the innovative nature of its rhythm section, and the prowess
of its soloists, and by 1945 the first two qualities had been
absorbed and built on by all ensembles which could do so.
The most encouraging and productive *milieu* for the innovative jazz soloist, on the other hand, soon became the small
ensemble.

The big bands, we should remember, were complex or-
ganizations, and for many of them the jazz-oriented instrumental pieces and the improvising soloist were only parts
of large repertoires—repertoires which also provided their
following with popular vocals and vocal groups, with the
latest hit ballads, with all sorts of dance music. Indeed, the
most successful bands—Tommy Dorsey's, for example—might
have not only staff composer-arranger-orchestrators but at
times even staff songwriters. In such a set-up, the jazz soloist and the occasional "band within the band" were elements necessary to success, but only elements.

Even before the final demise of the bands, aspects of their
music had broken off and become specialized pursuits: the
star pop singers of the 1940s and the improvising "bop"
quintets of the period carried on functions which, in the
1930s and 1940s, had often come in a single package.

By 1950, Count Basie was leading an octet and paying off
his debts, and if the opportunity was there in that group to
rediscover the Reno Club idiom or to find a new music for
a medium-sized ensemble, the challenge was not met. In-

deed, aside from an occasional soloist like Clark Terry, the players—or at least the solos—tended to be highly competent, proficient, and not much else. And the book tended to be familiar: the octet's *Tootie,* for instance, was a slick treatment of the blues called *Boogie Woogie (I May Be Wrong)* when it had been one of the earliest (and simplest) of the Reno Club "heads."

By mid-1951, Basie had re-formed and was leading an orchestra of four trumpets, three trombones, five saxophones, and four rhythm. As Leopold Stokowski knew as well as Paul Whiteman, every musician needs his public successes and his hits. The Basie ensemble quickly established itself, had some small success—*Little Pony, Paradise Squat, Cherry Point*—and soon had some larger ones—*Every Day* with singer Joe Williams; *April in Paris.* It also had an ensemble style quite unlike the Basie style of the 1930s and 1940s. Basie, who built his career on a spontaneity of spirit and the surprises of his soloists, re-established his career on precision, discipline, and mass effects. He soon had a unique, brass-oriented orchestra.

André Hodeir has described Basie's *April in Paris* as a treatment inappropriate for the piece and for the band. The arrangement is by "Wild Bill" Davis, who simply orchestrated his trio arrangement (electric organ, guitar, and drums) for Basie's band. I expect that this time Hodeir's sense of humor and his feel for the sublime, insightful irreverence in jazz failed him; perhaps the twice repeated "one more time" verbal ending of *April in Paris,* with its massive, relaxed response from the band, should have given him the clue.

Joe Williams's hits also give a clue to the nature of the new ensemble. When Jimmy Rushing gave the "call" of a blues line in the 1930s, the obligato response usually came from one of the star soloists. The response to Williams was apt to be a mass of muted brass and saxophones, voiced as one.

Joe Williams is apparently not a great spontaneous singer, and his ornaments and variations tend to be set—it seems—and repeated from performance to performance. But he possesses a sprightly, flexible, vocal instrument, and he introduces nuances and effects on his blues numbers that he has probably learned from his ballad singing—and they do not seem out of place. Joe Williams has extended the resources of the vocal blues.

By early 1956, the band had its masterpiece, a work by the saxophonist Frank Foster, one of the group's two tenor soloists, flippantly titled *Shiny Stockings*. The piece calls for the most relaxed precision, even to the nuances of "choked" and "swallowed" brass notes, and collective "shakes," underlined by the saxophonists. In *Shiny Stockings* Foster realized not only the range of precise ensemble effects the band was capable of, but also its power.

Hodeir has suggested that Foster's ensemble variations on *Shiny Stockings* are stronger than its theme, and if that is so, it seems a particularly appropriate quality for a major jazz work—more appropriate still for an ensemble leader who in mid-career had substituted the disciplined effects of his orchestra for the spontaneous abilities of his soloists.

I do not mean that the new Basie band did not have good soloists. There were the "two Franks," Foster and Wess, on tenor saxophones. Wess also played flute and thereby introduced a resource that remained a part of the Basie texture. Joe Newman was on trumpet, preserving a solo style from the earlier period. And there were Henry Coker, Benny Powell, and (later) Al Grey on trombone. I should also cite drummer Sonny Payne, who set the augmentive, interplaying percussive style which has become so much a part of this band's texture. The soloist of the highest calibre, how-

ever, was trumpeter Thad Jones, whose strong and individual talent was such that his departure in 1963 had perhaps
been delayed too long—but happily not before he had contributed the succinctly titled *Speaking of Sounds* to the
band's book.

If there is a stylistic precedent for this Basie band it was
the Jimmie Lunceford orchestra, the outstanding example
of a disciplined swing era ensemble, whose soloists were
functional parts of its music rather than equal partners or
its reason for being. Ironically, Lunceford's group, which
managed somehow to achieve its momentum in a "two-
beat" context, stubbornly ignored the democratization of
the beats that other ensembles had long since accomplished.

Frank Foster realized the power of the ensemble with a
masterpiece, *Shiny Stockings*. Others followed. Benny Carter, an important composer-arranger since the early 1930s
of course, provided a number of scores. Quincy Jones has
written well for the orchestra; indeed his *Jessica's Day*, originally conceived for Dizzy Gillespie, worked better for Basie.

It was Neal Hefti who heard the possibilities of a latent
and more subtle power, particularly in *Softly with Feeling*,
in the feature *Cute* for Frank Wess's flute and Sonny Payne's
wire brushes, and in the languid sentiments of *Li'l Darling*.
That last piece, incidentally, wasn't going well at the 1957
recording date which introduced it until the wife of record
producer Teddy Reig suggested they slow it down.

Surely if we had a brass group that could perform the baroque classics with the care, the discipline, and the collective joy that the Basie orchestra brings to its music, we would
have a generally celebrated musical treasure. But by saying
that I raise the further issue that, alas, in many people's
minds, such an ensemble as Basie's could prove itself only if
it were somehow to play Gabrieli the way it plays Foster
and Hefti. The later Basie orchestra would be eminently

worth hearing and worthy of high praise if its work were only an American "light music"—or even musical trash. But I think it played neither, and I venture to suggest that future generations may be puzzled to learn that our more eminent music journalists not only have not written about this remarkable ensemble, but apparently had not heard it.

As a final example of Basie's excellence, I recommend a 1959 arrangement by Ernie Wilkins, which has remained in the book. Wilkins used the group's power and its range of possible dynamics, from the leader's piano through the ensemble mass with unmuted brass on top. He put these resources to the same use as did Haydn in his *Surprise Symphony*. The arrangement also brings Basie's career full circle; for its recorded version, trumpeter Harry Edison, one of the original Basie soloists, returned to the orchestra. And the piece itself was the venerable *Moten Swing*. (*1982*)

Recordings

I cite recently available, domestic USA releases of the major recorded examples cited above. Titles not found herein have not received LP issue. And the dealers' import bins should always be consulted, particularly for Moten selections.

Basie's *In a Mellotone* is on Roulette SR 52028. And Basie's MCA 4050E collection includes *Jumpin' at the Woodside, Honeysuckle Rose,* and *Swinging the Blues.*

Jammin' for the Jackpot by Mills Blue Rhythm Band is included in New World NW 217. And Smithsonian Collection 2006 is a Fletcher Henderson set with *Honeysuckle Rose* and *Hot and Anxious.*

Verve MGV 8199 had the better version of *Shiny Stockings* and included Joe Williams on *Every Day. Li'l Darling* was on Roulette 4040, and *Moten Swing* on Roulette (S)R 52028.

Finally, one of the great losses to this band's recorded history is the poor recording quality and balance of its 1950s' Verve releases, including *Shiny Stockings, Every Day,* etc.

ع

GUITAR BY CHARLIE CHRISTIAN

Charlie Christian was not, as some commentators have contended, the first important jazz guitar soloist. Anyone who has heard Lonnie Johnson, with Louis Armstrong or with Duke Ellington or on his own, will know that he was not. Then there was Eddie Lang, an influence and object of respect in the 1920s and early 1930s, but whose work does not, in my opinion, survive its time. And there was—astonishing cultural development!—the Belgian-French gypsy, Django Reinhardt. Christian even had a predecessor or two on amplified guitar in Floyd Smith and Eddie Durham, the latter otherwise a well-known trombonist and composer-arranger.

But Christian was, in his brief career, not a major guitarist; he was *the* major guitarist and a major soloist regardless of instrument. Was and still is, for we have had several first-rate jazz guitarists since Christian, but none, I think, quite his equal. Anyone interested in jazz, the guitar, or the real achievements of American music should know his recordings.

Christian found a special style and special role for his special instrument, the amplified guitar. He knew the work of his predecessors, to be sure, but his major influences were the hornmen, more specifically the saxophonists, and most specifically Lester Young. He translated their influence into a single-string melodic technique—despite his rhythmic sureness and superb swing, he was not a chord-and-rhythm man, and, indeed, his best accompaniments were buoyant riffs of which he seemed to have an unending supply. His guitar style was, however, far from being merely imitative of a saxophone style, and his sound was a careful amplification of a personal guitar sound.

Christian was (according to a cliché of jazz history) a transitional figure between the jazz of the 1930s and the innovations of the 1940s. True, he was more harmonically exact and sophisticated than Lester Young, but, like Young, he remained as much a linear melodist. He was a great soloist by any standard; and in his short time before the public (Christian joined the Benny Goodman Sextet in late 1939 as an unknown and died a mere eighteen months later), he left a rich recorded heritage, not merely of excellent playing but of exceptional solos.

The typical Christian solo is organized in contrasts of brief, tight, riff figures and long, flowing bursts of lyric melody; and in his best improvisations these elements not only contrast effectively but also, paradoxically, lead one to another.

Christian's recorded heritage is not ideally served on current LP. About eleven years ago, Columbia reissued some of the Goodman performances (mono only, CL 652), which in a couple of cases were expanded by splicing in Christian solos from alternate, unused "takes." The Schwann catalogue still lists the album, so perhaps one can find it. One of Christian's masterpieces with Goodman, *I've Found a New Baby,* has never been on LP in the United States, but it is available on a CBS-Disque Christian album issued in Europe, *"Solo Flight"* (62-581), which is worth obtaining.

There are still available the invaluable jam sessions recordings, the only ones we have (Archive of Folk and Jazz Music 219), which feature Christian's chorus-after-chorus inventiveness on several pieces.

The foregoing words are prompted by the appearance of
a Blue Note album, *"Celestial Express"* (B-6505), which re-
issues two sessions from the 1940s led by clarinetist Edmond
Hall.

The second comes from 1944 and is, in a sense, an ersatz
Goodman small-group date, with generally good work from
Red Norvo, a very good solo by Teddy Wilson on *Smooth
Sailin',* and, on the slow *Blue Interval,* excellent work by
Wilson and two superb improvisations by Hall.

The earlier session represented on *"Celestial Express"*
comes from 1941 and is a quartet with an unusual instrumentation, in which Hall's clarinet is joined by Meade
"Lux" Lewis on celeste, Charlie Christian on unamplified
guitar, and Israel Crosby on bass for a program of blues at
various tempos.

Individually, the players do well. However, on the faster
pieces, the instrumentation itself risks a kind of thumping,
stringed heaviness in the rhythm section which the high,
belled tones of the celeste could not temper as a piano
would. Still, Christian has a good solo on *Jammin' in Four,*
and the take-your-turn, solo-and-accompaniment counterpoint of Lewis and Hall on *Edmond Hall Blues* is very
good.

However, everything—instrumentation, sonorities, style,
players—comes together on *Profoundly Blue.* It opens with
three superb Christian choruses, with Crosby in a true
countermelody behind him, and with a few gently ren-
dered comments from Lewis as well. It is a performance of
such exceptional musical and emotional quality as to produce a sense of sustained wonder, both the first time one

hears it and the hundredth. There is even a second "take" of *Profoundly Blue* included, but its excellences only serve to dramatize the magic quality of the first.

Happily, the LP transfer of this Blue Note reissue has been done without phony electronic stereo, but there is a bit of surface noise that was not audible on an early ten-inch LP issue of some of this material.   (*1969*)

I have left the record references in the preceding essay as they were as of 1969. Subsequently, Columbia Records issued a two-record set of Christian with the Goodman Sextet (CG-30779) which, again, involved some unissued material. Included was *I've Found a New Baby,* but, alas, not in the classic "take" but only in an alternate. Much Christian broadcast material has also appeared on "collectors" labels. And on Jazz Archives JA-6 there was a remarkable unissued Goodman Sextet session, with Christian and Lester Young, plus Count Basie, Buck Clayton, Jo Jones—altogether exceptional music with Young playing in middle range and with harmonic care as nowhere else on his early recordings. (*1984*)

ᘒ᷍

ELLA AND HER CRITICS

Ella Fitzgerald, as you may know, is a singer's singer. Her control is sure, her notes are clear, her pitch is precise. Her range isn't wide but her voice has body, perhaps as much body as a popular singer is entitled to. Her rhythm is impeccable. And she swings, still in the manner of her beginning, *circa* 1936. But for all her professional control she can improvise and her final chorus or so may give impressions of a gleeful abandon.

Ella Fitzgerald is also the public's singer. She packs them in at the record shops, auditoriums, and night clubs. But she is not, as you may not know, a reviewer's singer—at least not in some quarters.

Her Verve release, V/V6-4060, is in her series of "songbook" sets and is devoted to the work of that displaced American-Viennese, Jerome Kern. Her accompaniment was arranged by Nelson Riddle, who writes with a good understanding of Ella Fitzgerald, with miraculously relevant taste in scoring for strings, and with the same coy brass figures that he has been using for the past ten years. As her detractors protest, Miss Fitzgerald often does ignore the words to her songs. (So much the better for her, perhaps?) One thing she responds to, in her relatively uncluttered way, is harmony. It is a response that Kern's pieces can only encourage and that Riddle understands, as witness the cumulative, modulative climax he provides for her on *A Fine Romance.* Also, without any egocentric connotations, Ella Fitzgerald responds to the quality of her own voice and to the paradox of its precision plus its slight natural hoarseness. Hear her first chorus to *All the Things You Are,* or hear the way she undertakes the difficult steps on *Remind Me.* She is also a good spontaneous, original melodist; again, listen to her second version of the release, the middle part of *All the Things You Are.* Or notice how agreeable she makes the cutie-pie aspect of Kern when she recomposes *She Didn't Say Yes.*

No, Ella Fitzgerald is not capable of tragedy. She is capable of good introspective melodrama (*Yesterdays*) and of a kind of nostalgic pensiveness (*Can't Help Lovin' That Man*). To her detractors, all the rest is engaging shallowness. But for me, hers is the stuff of joy, a joy that is profound and ever replenished—perhaps from the self-discovery that, for all her equipment as a singer's singer, she is absolutely incapable of holding anything back. (*1964*)

The general level of Ella Fitzgerald's recordings before 1966 was so high that one might recommend almost any of them to the novice Fitzgerald listener. But certainly from her earlier years, the first Gershwin collection, with only Ellis Larkins's piano as her accompaniment, remains classic American recorded song. And *Ella Hums the Blues* seems to me a neglected classic from among all her early wordless "scat" vocalese performances. The former was last reissued on MCA 215E. The latter did reappear as a part of an MCA issue of the earlier *"Lullabies of Birdland"* LP. Perhaps that issue can still be found; or perhaps *Ella Hums the Blues* also appears in one of the "best of Ella Fitzgerald" volumes which MCA issues periodically.

Even within the pre-1966 catalogue there is a distinction to be made. I have never seen it said in print, but the mid-1950s were a turning point for almost all American vernacular singers: they ceased to croon and began to sing with fuller voice. Compare Frank Sinatra on Columbia with Sinatra on Capitol after 1953. Compare Ella Fitzgerald on Gershwin, as recommended above, with Ella Fitzgerald on the longer Gershwin set she later did for Verve.

For that same Verve label, she did her *tour de force* of scat, an astonishing, extended *Take the "A" Train* in an album called *"Ella in Hollywood"* (Verve V6-4052, also catalogued as Polygram 340).

But of all of Fitzgerald's "song book" albums, by far the most consistent is the Harold Arlen collection (recently reissued as Verve 817-526): an almost perfect meeting of talents in the composer (there was more jazz in Arlen than in any of our other great songwriters, Gershwin included), the singer, and arranger Billy May, who showed fine sensitivity to the singer and a greater rare taste in *his* occasional use of strings than Riddle did on the Kern set discussed above. And the Arlen set has a *Blues in the Night* on which Ella Fitzgerald and her accompanists display a sense of sustained high drama that make it perhaps the classic of all her recorded performances.

I have twice mentioned the year 1966 above as a kind of cut-off date. It was in that year that age and use began to take its toll on Ella Fitzgerald's voice, a voice, and a singer's art, in which the aforementioned clarity and purity and control of pitch were central and crucial. That is a sad judgment to have to record, and a sad and painful loss for American music. (*1984*)

ॐ

WHAT DOES A JAZZ COMPOSER DO?*

I

Jazz is a player's idiom, a performer's music. It is also a music that borrows much of its repertory from the tradition of American popular songwriting and from the indigenous Afro-American blues. And it is a music in which the player is supposed to extemporize, to improvise much of what he plays as he goes along. What possible place could a composer have in such music? What function does he fulfill?

* This essay combines portions of "Jazz Composition: What Is It?" which appeared in *Down Beat* and "And What Might a Jazz Composer Do?" from the *Music Educators Journal*.

These questions can be answered in several ways, the first of which has to do with the jazz player himself. The great jazz improvisers are themselves spontaneous composers of melody. Leonard Bernstein once said that jazz musicians "play with notes," but they do far more than that. Guitarist Charlie Christian's spontaneous chorus on *I Found a New Baby* or alto saxophonist Charlie Parker's *Embraceable You* variations are not simply a succession of notes or fanciful musical phrases strung together. They are subtly organized instrumental melodies, and they go quite beyond their points of departure in the popular repertory. The heritage of recorded jazz abounds in such outstanding improvised melodies.

Christian's and Parker's solos are, of course, harmonic variations, melodic inventions oriented in the chord progressions of their respective popular songs. Nowadays, contemporary jazz offers the soloist fewer protections. Often it rejects a chord progression or outline as a basis for improvisation, and the soloist uses a scale or mode instead, allowing him a free-form approach to phrasing and structure. Despite this departure, such solos as Miles Davis's *So What* or Ornette Coleman's *Congeniality* are commendable examples of spontaneous instrumental melody.

What about embellishmental variations? What about jazz soloists who, in part or in whole, use a melodically oriented, ornamental style? Such solos are not, in the strict eighteenth-century sense of the term, improvisations, and performances like Art Tatum's remarkably rich *Willow Weep for Me* or Thelonious Monk's starkly beautiful *I Should Care* might be called ornamental interpretations of standard popular melodies. But in view of the striking harmonic originality of each man's performance and the complex nature of each man's treatment of the melody—in Tatum's case by complex ornamentation and rephrasing of the original, in Monk's by simplification and distillation—it might be more useful to say that each pianist has re-composed the work in question. Each man, furthermore, has transformed a song and its accompaniment into an integrated work for keyboard, discovering hidden beauties and implications otherwise undreamed of.

There is a further kind of jazz performance (another kind of re-composition, if you will) that is neither outright invention nor outright ornamentation, but a little of each. For such performances, the French jazz critic André Hodeir has borrowed the rhetorician's term *paraphrase*. Louis Armstrong was a magician of this idiom; he alternated fragments of the original with inventions of his own—anticipating some notes and phrases, delaying others, changing note values, and creating rich melody from ordinary popular ditties like the ripely sentimental *Sweethearts on Parade* as well as from very good popular songs, as in his eloquent simplification of Harold Arlen's *I Gotta Right To Sing the Blues*.

Other jazz performers have been masters of such paraphrase and re-composition by paraphrase. One thinks immediately of one of Armstrong's great stylistic followers, the singer Billie Holiday (and, indeed, of most of the great jazz singers); of vibraphonist Milt Jackson, who excels at both paraphrase and invention; and of Fats Waller and Erroll Garner, particularly, among pianists.

II

Charlie Parker was, then, one of the great jazz improvisers. He also contributed many durable pieces to the jazz repertory. But Charlie Parker was not a great jazz composer.

His pieces were melodic lines, lines most frequently written to fit chord changes that were already there, borrowed from popular songs that had become jazz standards. *Scrapple from the Apple,* one of his best melodies, began with the chords of *Honeysuckle Rose,* with the bridge from *I Got Rhythm.* It is possible to write poor lines on preset chords, and it is possible to write good ones, but in either case, one is contributing only a succession of melody notes.

Parker's best piece is *Confirmation,* a most delightful and ingenious melody. For one thing, it is a continuous linear invention. Most pop songs and many jazz pieces have two parts, a main strain and a bridge, or middle strain. The main strain is repeated twice before the bridge and once after it. *Confirmation* skips along beautifully with no repeats (except for one very effective echo phrase) until the last eight bars, which are a kind of repeat-in-summary.

Moreover, the bridge does not seem an interruption or an interlude that breaks up the flow of the piece but is a part of the continuously developing melody. Finally, if the chord sequence to *Confirmation* preceded the melody, then the melody became so strong as Parker worked on it that it forced him to alter the chords to fit its developing contours. *Confirmation* is Parker's approach to what is usually called composition.

And again, composition is, in some sense, a piece for instruments. It is not for voice—not a "song."

In its early stages, music begins as rhythm and then becomes vocal melody. But when man begins to use musical instruments, even simple drums, he discovers that the instruments have characteristics and resources the human voice does not have. Songs are written for the voice. The more able and trained the voice gets, the more complex the songs can become. But—to give a rule of thumb—we write compositions for the specific resources of musical instruments.

The best test is that when we have heard a good song, we are likely to come away singing it ourselves. But when we have heard a good composition, we want to hear the instruments play it again. That explanation is not absolute, of course, because there are plenty of good instrumental melodies that we can sing or hum, and there are plenty of good songs that composers have been able to orchestrate effectively.

Jazz, like any other music, began as rhythm and then became song and chant. And soon this song and chant were imitated on homemade and "legitimate" instruments.

Apparently the whole intention of the early jazz player, as nearly as it can be deduced, was to imitate the human voice. At about the turn of the century, however, there developed a style called ragtime. Many ragtime melodies were derived from songs of various sources, but ragtime was primarily an instrumental music. At first it was a piano music, and simple, optimistic ragtime melodies had a definite instrumental conception, partly because ragtime was heavily influenced by march music.

Ragtime made a contribution in instrumental melody to jazz that is still being felt. However, improvisation is not primary to ragtime, and even written variation is comparatively rare. But a ragtime piece is a two-handed composition for piano in which the melody and the harmony exist together.

Take the first really good rag, Scott Joplin's *Maple Leaf Rag*. The melody has little meaning by itself, and, despite their simplicity, the chord changes belong intrinsically to it. In his later years, in a piece like *Euphonic Sounds,* Joplin tried to extend the idiom further so that the left hand did not simply make rhythms and harmonies but was given an interweaving melodic function as well.

III

An orchestral composer in the European sense is not simply a melodist nor even just a harmonist. He is also an orchestrator and a musical architect. Theme, treatment, and structure are all one in his work. The same is true of the great jazz composers. Since they work with an improvisational music, however, jazz composers must also take into account what is contributed by the ensemble and by the individual, what is established beforehand and what is made up in performance.

Three great jazz composers who have been such architects are Ferdinand Morton (better known, of course, as "Jelly Roll"), Duke Ellington, and Thelonious Monk. Each man's music represents a quite different approach to the same problems and, therefore, different solutions.

There are some interesting similarities among these men. Each is a pianist. Each also has been called a poor pianist—which, in some irrelevant way, each may be. Each man, in having an orchestral conception of piano and in terms of the specific techniques of jazz (techniques that jazz does *not* necessarily have in common with other music), is actually a kind of jazz virtuoso. Each also has, in his own way, a concern for over-all form in a performance. That concern goes beyond composition to include exactly the way the soloist is related to the piece and to the total effect of a performance.

Monk, for example, is not interested in finger dexterity. But in terms of unique sound; of the most subtle sense of rhythm, meter, accent, and time; of the musical worth of each melody note and each note in each chord; of the ability to find endless and fascinating variations on even the simplest idea, Monk is one of the great jazzmen.

Structurally, Jelly Roll Morton's music is derived from ragtime, which is to say from a kind of Afro-American polka or Sousa-styled march music that uses several themes with effective tonal, melodic, and melodic-rhythmic relationships among them. Morton brought to ragtime structure a new, more fluid rhythmic concept, and he added variations, sometimes written but more often improvised.

One of Morton's best recordings is of a piece he called *Dead Man Blues*. Like W. C. Handy's blues, and like ragtime pieces before them, *Dead Man* is built on several themes. These themes obviously need to work well together; they can't be three handy melodies just thrown into the same piece. And they need to be put into some kind of order that gives a musical and emotional development.

In orchestration one concern of the composer is to decide who plays what, who improvises when, and how to bring out the best in the improviser without letting him overpower the whole performance. The whole, in an ideal performance of a great jazz composition, has to be greater than the sum of its parts.

Morton's recording of *Dead Man* begins with the echo of a funeral, in an introductory bit of Chopin's *Funeral March*, played on trombone with just the merest hint of humor.

From this point on *Dead Man* attempts the very difficult task of being sober—even reverent—and at the same time being spirited. The first theme in *Dead Man* is stated in a dancing polyphony by the trumpet's lead, with the clarinet quietly in a second melody behind it, and a trombone in a rhythmic-melodic bass line. There is a wonderful lightness of melody and sound and rhythm in this chorus. It is quite unlike the heavy, plodding, and strident Dixieland ensembles we so often hear nowadays. Such masterful ensemble playing in the style is perhaps a lost art.

The second section of *Dead Man* is a series of variations. The first is a chorus by Omer Simeon's clarinet. In the second, trumpeter George Mitchell shapes two lovely, logically developed, simple melodies. Mitchell's second chorus is also a contrast to his first and it further prepares for the entrance of the third *Dead Man* theme. It is rare that a solo can have such structural uses and still be beautiful in itself, but the great jazz composers can always encourage such playing.

The third part of *Dead Man* begins simply, with a trio of clarinets playing a lovely, rifflike blues line. As they repeat it, Kid Ory's trombone enters behind them with a deeply sung countermelody. In the next chorus, actually a return to the opening theme, as if encouraged by Ory, Mitchell and Simeon join the trombonist; the other two clarinets drop out. The three horns play another lovely three-part variation on that opening theme. Obviously, this section also echoes the polyphonic chorus with which the record began, and it beautifully balances the piece with a similar effect at beginning and end.

Morton's best records abound with effects. Pieces like *Black Bottom Stomp, Grampa's Spells, Kansas City Stomps* have harmony, polyphony, solo, stop-time breaks, alternating 2/4 and 4/4 time, have rhythm instruments dropping out and re-entering, call-and-response patterns, riffs—*Smoke House Blues* even has a sudden double-time on top of a double-time.

Such a catalogue of devices may make Morton's records sound ridiculously cluttered, particularly when it is remembered that most of them use two or three themes. But they are not. They move from beginning to end with a rare purpose, direction, and order.

IV

Duke Ellington was the jazz composer par excellence. To many of us, indeed, he was and is the great American composer, regardless of category. He used the dance band as a means of personal expression, and many of his best works are therefore instrumental miniatures, conceived within the conventions of American dance music but executed as works of high musical art.

In his orchestrations, and most particularly in his individual voicings, Ellington proved himself to be one of the most original harmonic thinkers of this century. And through instrumental doublings on the part of his reed players, through ingenious combinations of instruments, and through the carefully crafted uses of mutes on the part of his brass players, he achieved a rich variety of sonorities and textures from his ensemble—which numbered as few as ten musicians in his early years.

Ellington learned a great deal from his immediate predecessors and contemporaries—chiefly from Fletcher Henderson—about how to transform the jazz-influenced American dance band (with its reed, brass, and rhythm sections) into a true jazz orchestra. But it was not until he encountered nightclub "show" work, with its call for overtures, choruses, and specialty dance accompaniments, and the other demands of the miniature musical "review" these establishments featured, that his genius began to show itself. He made his dance band into a show band, and his show band a vehicle for a collaborative yet personal musical expression.

Ellington worked with the individual talents of his musicians in the same way that the great dramatists of the past have worked with their actors or the great ballet masters have worked with their dancers. Indeed, his harmonic originality itself was dictated not so much in the abstract but by, let us say, how this player's A-flat sounded, and how it in turn might sound when juxtaposed with another man's highly individual G in his upper register.

In his outstanding study *Jazz: Its Evolution and Essence,* Hodeir calls Ellington's *Ko-ko* one of his most important compositions and a work of "freshness and serenity . . . breadth and grandeur." *Ko-ko* is a two-theme, twelve-measure blues in a minor key. It features trombonist Joe Nanton (the soulful artist with the plunger mute who gave the early Ellington ensemble so much of its characteristic sound), with valve trombonist Juan Tizol and bassist Jimmy Blanton also heard briefly in solo parts. *Ko-ko* is the sort of performance that repays the most careful chorus-by-chorus, phrase-by-phrase examination of the sort we gave Morton's *Grandpa's Spells.* But with *Ko-ko,* there are greater rewards to be gleaned from attention to the sonorities and textures, and greater rewards still from an examination of Ellington's voicings.

Tizol's opening antiphonal statements on *Ko-ko* are purely interpretive, with perhaps some embellishmental leeway allowed him. Nanton's solo, which first introduces *Ko-ko*'s second section or theme, was undoubtedly his own improvisation at its inception, but, once arrived at, it was played verbatim or interpretively or with embellishment— whichever the trombonist chose in a given performance. On the other hand, the solos on so carefully wrought an Ellington piece as *Harlem Air Shaft,* or on so loosely conceived a performance as *In a Mellotone,* might come out differently from one performance to the next without destroying either the identity or the unity of either work.

The composer has variously provided theme statements, a chord progression, antiphonal figures and accompaniment figures, counterpoint, ensemble variations, and recapitulations, and these remain constant. If the soloist understands these and their function, and is willing to work within the mood or substance of the piece, he may choose his notes and phrases and build his melodies quite differently in a given interpretation.

By contrast, a first-rate big-band blues from the same period, like Count Basie's *One O'Clock Jump,* belongs to each soloist in turn, and then to the group for a wrap-up that is again almost a-thing-in-itself. Ellington's *Main Stem* belongs to its composer, to its soloists, and to the group throughout.

V

If any jazz composer can be said to have surpassed Ellington in any respect whatever, it probably is Thelonious Monk in the uniquely instrumental conception and spontaneous character of certain of his pieces. In Monk's best music, one again hears the mind and guidance of the composer at work. Yet in the little quartets and quintets with which Monk usually works, form and structure are themselves apt to be spontaneous and arrived at in the act of performance itself, not premeditated and written like Ellington's.

Misterioso, for example, is a twelve-measure blues, performed (in Monk's best recorded version) by a quartet consisting of vibraharp (Milt Jackson), piano (Monk), string bass (John Simmons), and drums (Shadow Wilson). Monk's blues theme is stated in the opening chorus by Monk and Jackson in unison, as the bass and drums phrase along with the two keyboards. The melody here is typical Monkian transmutation of an indigenous "walking" blues bass line in sixths, an example of traditional material personally reassessed and brought up to date.

With the second chorus, Jackson begins to improvise on the blues, and the bass and drums go into a regular 4/4 jazz "walk" in accompaniment. Monk, however, does not "feed" Jackson blues chords in the standard manner of accompaniment. He improvises a kind of orchestrator's counterpoint based on a stark, spare use of the "blue seventh," the next implied note of his theme, if you will. It is as though Monk were saying, "This is not just blues being played in this key. This is *my* blues piece called *Misterioso*."

Monk's own solo, following Jackson's, uses ascending phrases that echo the upward movement of his theme. And as Jackson begins a reprise of the *Misterioso* melody at the end of the performance, Monk at first does not join him, but scatters contrapuntal fragments beneath him. These fragments echo Monk's former accompaniment to the vibraharpist, plus hints of phrases from the pianist's own solo. Finally, there is a joining in unison with Jackson on the theme. Thus Monk, through a tissue of provocative phrases and fragments, summarizes the whole performance in its final chorus and affirms its subtle unity.

Monk had to wait a long time to become known, but he wrote and had recorded *Criss Cross, Four in One, Skippy, Gallop's Gallop, Epistrophy, Evidence* (which *does* have a borrowed chord progression); and *Misterioso* before fame overtook him.

VI

Like Monk, John Lewis works with materials that seem simple on the surface. One of his best pieces, for example, is *The Golden Striker*, which might be called a somewhat modernized *Bugle Call Rag*, using the chords to the *King*

Porter Stomp. Another Lewis achievement is the blues *Two Degrees East, Three Degrees West.* It sounds quite traditional and simple perhaps, but it has highly original twists of phrasing in its compellingly logical melody.

Lewis's best single piece is undoubtedly *Django,* and the Modern Jazz Quartet's performances of it are among the really sustained "extended" small-group jazz performances on records.

The gradations of feeling in *Django* are also exceptional. It is of course, a memorial to guitarist Django Reinhardt, and its main theme suggests a French gypsy, a guitarist, and jazz, all at once.

It also is a funeral piece. And hovering in the background is the New Orleans tradition that funerals become occasions for rejoicing and reaffirmation of life as well as of reverent sadness. Besides its theme, *Django* is a chord sequence for the improvisers and not the same as that of the main theme. There is also a little recurring bass figure that is probably as old as jazz and that was used in King Oliver's 1926 blues *Snag It.*

One really successful Lewis piece that has been performed outside the MJQ is *Three Little Feelings,* written for a brass orchestra and Miles Davis.

In jazz composition since Monk, however, the ideal is that the act of playing a piece and playing variations on it become one unbroken line. The soloist is almost forced to re-compose every piece in playing it, and the theme and variations assume a kind of equal status.

One is reminded of Charlie Mingus, for, similarly, some of Mingus's best pieces *are* the performances of such pieces.

One cannot imagine *Pithecanthropus Erectus* or *Haitian Fight Song* or *Folk Forms* aside from performance. It is as if the performance gave the composition whatever existence it has. A question like, "How does *Pithecanthropus* go?" is meaningless—it goes the way it is played, and only that way. Composition and collecitve performance are one.

Mingus often laments not having had a big band to work with all the time. But with achievements like *Pithecanthropus* and *Fight Song,* one wonders. Jazz would be poorer without them. *(1962/1975)*

ತಿⵦ

IN MEMORIAM,
BUD POWELL

Pianist Earl "Bud" Powell died the night of August 1, 1966, in Kings County Hospital, New York. The obituaries mentioned tuberculosis, malnutrition, and alcoholism, but it might be said that Bud Powell died of something—a demon perhaps—that pursued him most of his life and that manifested itself in symptoms that were sometimes physical and sometimes psychological. Or perhaps Bud Powell died of the scarred, unreachably tragic nature of his own being and of the terrible buffeting that life had given him.

By the mid-forties, it was fairly common among insiders to say that Powell on piano was to the modern jazz of the time what Dizzy Gillespie was on trumpet and Charlie Parker on alto saxophone. Musically, he had followed a lead that they provided, to be sure, but to put it that he was "Bird on piano" is to overlook his pianistic heritage, which included an assimilation of (among others) Art Tatum and Teddy Wilson. It is also to overlook his own contributions; his most immediately obvious debt to Parker and

Gillespie was that he had absorbed them rhythmically, but clearly he spoke their language with accents and punctuations of his own.

Within a few years some of his ideas had received the idle flattery of middle-brow popularization by George Shearing. But Powell also received the deeper compliments of a more legitimate following among a whole generation of younger pianists. "They cut him up like a gathering of anxious medical students working on a corpse," remarked one player in the early fifties, and many of them took what they could and played it the best they could. Certainly no one equaled the master. Horace Silver was one who understood that it was best not to try, but rather to take what one could and make something of one's own.

Powell sometimes played like a man running before a threat, and perhaps a part of him knew from the beginning that time would run out for him. There was an urgency in his playing that was sometimes almost extra-musical and sometimes not, and there was a hard, emphatic precision in his touch, even at the fleetest tempos, that was, and has remained, entirely his own.

Powell's style belonged to the mid-forties, as does his heritage, and the best of his recordings were made by 1953. The great Powell is not the faintly pretentious composer who wrote *Glass Enclosure* out of Prokofiev, or who translated his youthful exercises into *Bud on Bach,* or who came up with an effective Latin-esque novelty in *Un Poco Loco.* Nor is it the Powell of slow ballads—the shadow of Tatum lingered across his keyboard all too often in such moods. The great Powell is the Powell of medium and fast tempo pieces from the modern repertory such as *Ornithology, A Night in Tunisia, Little Benny* (which in his version is called *Bud's Bubble*), *Tempus Fugit, 52nd Street Theme, Parisian Thoroughfare,* or the Powell of standard melodies at similar tempos such as *I'll Remember April, Somebody Loves Me, All God's Children Got Rhythm,* or *Indiana.*

Intricate structures to him weren't all-important; he found inspiration in both sophisticated outlines (*How High the Moon*) and simple ones (the blues, and *I Got Rhythm*). His reharmonization of, say, *I Want To Be Happy* is both unassuming and ingenious, but what usually mattered in Powell's playing was his finding a basis, almost *any* basis, for his own inventive, linear energy, an energy that seemed both unabated and, one might say, insatiable. Melodies simply seemed to cascade out of him. But under inspection they prove to be logical melodies.

There is an astonishing moment on his first version of *A Night in Tunisia* where his right hand winds through a sustained linkage of notes for a full eight measures, unbroken by a single rest or bar line, but there is nothing of a technical stunt involved in that passage. Nor is there anything greatly exceptional about it, and, symbolically at least, the moment is characteristic Powell. It is also so musical that (as with many another of his improvised lines) if it were transcribed, slowed down, and played quietly, it would prove to have a natural lyricism that is both surprising and fundamental to its character.

Powell made, as time has already witnessed, too many records, and some of them are painful to hear. When he was ill, the otherwise precise, galvanized coordination of his hands was not there, and he seemed not to know it. And, toward the end, he made some recordings where the separate techniques of each hand had deteriorated. But throughout the fifties and into the sixties there were brief, heartening, but ultimately frustrating recoveries, when the old technique and creativity came back to him.

The best Powell is contained in two Blue Note albums

called *"The Amazing Bud Powell"* (81503 and 81504); in
his Roost album, *"The Bud Powell Trio"* (2224); and two
Verve albums, *"Bud Powell: Jazz Giant"* (8153) and *"The
Genius of Bud Powell,"* recently collected as Verve 2506.
Powell as a member of a Charlie Parker Quintet partici-
pated in some of Parker's Savoy recordings (last collected
as Savoy 5500). (*1966*)

ᘒ

HONORING BILL EVANS*

Several times pianist William John Evans spoke publicly of
a singular moment when he first discovered the freedom
that goes with being a jazz player. And several times also he
spoke of the enormous requisite discipline that went with it.

About the freedom, he was playing as a pre-teenager with
a dance band in his home state of New Jersey. The group
was doing *Tuxedo Junction,* a piece which was originally
produced and performed in an atmosphere of improvisation in the Eskine Hawkins band, and in most of the other
big swing bands that later adopted it. But by the time
Tuxedo Junction had become a dance-band "stock" arrangement, the parts had been simplified, locked in, and
ready to be read off the paper.

"For some reason," Evans said, "I got inspired to put in
a little blues thing. *Tuxedo Junction* is in B-flat, and I put
in a little D-flat, D, F thing, bing! in the right band. It was
such a thrill. It sounded right and good, and it wasn't writ-

* Adapted and condensed from the notes to Fantasy's boxed set, *"The Complete Bill Evans Riverside Recordings"* (R018).

ten, and I had done it. The idea of doing something in music that somebody hadn't thought of opened a whole new world to me."

On the question of the discipline that is a part of the equipment of any great improviser, Evans spoke often. Even on the most uninspired occasion, on the most uninspiring job, he once explained, he could approach the bandstand with no hope of having anything good in him to play, and the accumulated discipline of knowing how to make his mind and hands and feet respond when the inspiration did come, that discipline itself would simply take over and let—even *cause*—the flow of musical ideas to be there.

When the Bill Evans Trio was formed in 1959 the leader said that he hoped it would "grow in the direction of simultaneous improvisation rather than just one guy blowing followed by another guy blowing. If the bass player, for example, hears an idea that he wants to answer, why should he just keep playing a 4/4 background? The men I'll work with have learned how to do the regular kind of playing, and so I think we now have the license to change it. After all, in a classical composition, you don't hear a part remain stagnant until it becomes a solo. There are transitional development passages—a voice begins to be heard more and more and finally breaks into prominence.

"Especially, I want my work (and the trio's if possible) to sing. I want to play what I like to hear. I'm not going to be strange or new just to be strange or new. If what I do grows that way naturally, that'll be O.K. But it must have that wonderful feeling of singing."

It is perhaps up to commentators like me to point out that the Trio's bassist, Scott LaFaro, was then moving jazz bass along the lines that it had been going for some time— with Charlie Mingus outlining the way—and that he was doing it with an irresistible virtuosity. The mono version of

Autumn Leaves from the Trio's first studio date and the original take of *Blue in Green* are the initial masterpieces in just the kind of three-way performances Evans had hoped for.

Bill Evans could have been a major musician-critic. Indeed, if we were to collect all he wrote and said about the music and its players, he might appear to have been just that.

Take the notes he contributed to the seminal Miles Davis *"Kind of Blue"* LP (1959). Evans compared "the extremely severe and unique disciplines of the jazz or improvising musician" to the art of the spontaneous watercolorists of Japan, who paint on a thin parchment "in such a way that an unnatural or interrupted stroke will destroy the line or break through the parchment. Erasures or changes are impossible. These artists must practice a particular discipline, that of allowing the idea to express itself in communication with their hands in such a direct way that deliberation cannot interfere."

The pictures that result, he added, may "lack the complex composition and textures of ordinary painting, but it is said that those who will see will find something captured that escapes explanation."

Or take the comments Evans wrote for one of Thelonious Monk's Columbia LPs. He called Monk "an exceptionally uncorrupted creative talent," who was largely uninfluenced by any musical tradition except that of American popular music and jazz. Monk had, against huge conformist pressures, replaced formal superficialities with "fundamental structure" and produced "a unique and astoundingly pure music which combined aptitude, insight, drive, compassion, fantasy and whatever else makes a total artist."

Or these words on Miles Davis's development (from an

interview in *Contemporary Keyboard* in 1981): "[He is] an example of somebody I think was a late arriver, even though he was recorded when he first came on the scene. You can hear how consciously he was soloing and how his knowledge was a very aware thing. He just constantly kept working and contributing to his own craft. . . . And then at one point it all came together and he emerged with maturity, and he became a total artist and influence, making a kind of beauty that has never been heard before or since."

But like any important artist-critic, Evans was, in no self-serving way, also speaking of himself, his own struggles and growth, whenever he discussed others.

His remarks on Monk's commitment to the jazz and popular traditions, for instance, were a comment on Evans. "I believe in the language of the popular idiom," he said later, "and this has come out of not just our culture but all of history, especially the traditional jazz idiom. It is the experience of millions of people and of conditions which are impossible to take into consideration. . . . Now if I could take the feelings and experience I have from this traditional idiom and somehow extend it to another area of expression . . . I want everything to have roots."

His comments on Miles Davis were a part also of one of the most succinct of his many comments on the need for discipline and (most important) his insistence on the need for the artist to arrive at his own best style, the one that would allow for a continued artistic growth and development. Indeed, this seems to me one of the most perceptive statements in all the literature of jazz: "I always like people who have developed long and hard, especially through introspection and a lot of dedication. I think what they arrive at is usually . . . deeper and more beautiful . . . than the person who seems to have that ability and fluidity from the beginning. I say this because it's a good message to give to

young talents who feel as I used to. You hear musicians playing with great fluidity and complete conception early on,
and you don't have that ability. I didn't. I had to know
what I was doing. And yes, ultimately it turned out that
these people weren't able to carry their thing very far. I
found myself being more attracted to artists who have developed through the years and become better and deeper
musicians."

That need to know what he was doing, intellectually,
theoretically, was one pull of the dichotomy of this remarkable combination of careful deliberateness and intuitive
spontaneity, of logic and sensitivity, mind and heart, that
was Bill Evans the musician. He elaborated—in a singular
account of a musical self-education—to Don DeMichael in
the introduction to the music folio *Bill Evans Plays*. "I
think it was a good thing I didn't have a great aptitude for
mimicry, though it made it very difficult for me at the time
because I had to build my whole musical style. I'd abstract
musical principles from the people I dug, and I'd take their
feeling or technique to apply to things the way that I'd
built them. But because I had to build them meticulously,
I think worked out better in the end because it gave me a
complete understanding of everything I was doing."

"I don't want to express just my feelings," he told De-
Michael, "—all my feelings aren't interesting to everybody . . ."

In view of Evans's commitment to the American popular
song as his major vehicle—a subject we shall return to—his
recording called *Peace Piece;* his superb "free" solo on
George Russell's *All About Rosie;* and his participation in
the Davis LP *"Kind of Blue"* call for special comment.
These events either lead to, or were early parts of, the
movement variously called "modal" jazz or "free" jazz. And

they were efforts on the part of jazz musicians to find new bases for improvising, after they had explored basically the same bases for over thirty-five years.

Of *Peace Piece,* Evans said at the time, "It's completely free form. I just had one figure that gave the piece a tonal reference and a rhythmic reference. Thereafter, everything could happen over that one solid thing. Except for the bass figure, it was a complete improvisation. We did it in two takes. Because it was totally improvised," he added "I so far haven't been able to do it again when I've been asked for it in clubs."

Peace Piece, like *Flamenco Sketches* on the *"Kind of Blue"* album, is conceived as a succession of scales which the soloist takes up one at a time, improvises on for as long as he pleases, and then turns to the next. The notes available to the improviser are a "given," but the structure, phrase length, and the overall length are spontaneous.

Blue in Green was also on *"Kind of Blue."* It was written by Evans on a succession of unusually juxtaposed chords apparently suggested to him by Miles Davis, and on a ten-measure, rather than twelve-measure, phrase. Strictly speaking, *Blue in Green* is neither "free" nor "modal," but it is very challenging to the player, requiring him to get gracefully as well as correctly from one chord to the next and "think" in phrases of unusual length.

And just for the record, the other highly influential piece on *"Kind of Blue," So What,* is opposite to *Flamenco Sketches,* but is like the flowing *Milestones.* Phrased like an AABA popular song, the piece gives the player 16 measures of one scale (or mode), eight of another, then back to eight of the first. In other words, he's got the notes to choose from and his phrase lengths assigned, but no assigned chords to wend his way through.

However, it was Evans's left hand chord voicings that had

the widest effect on other musicians, and they are not too difficult to explain to the layman. Bill *voiced* certain chords, that is, he chose the notes to go in those chords, leaving out the "root" notes. The roots tie down the chord and its sound. Without them, a given chord can sometimes have several identities; it can lead easily, consonantly to a wider choice of other chords; and it can accommodate a wider choice of melody notes and phrases for the player on top of the chords. The "open" voicings that Bill used opened up melody and flow in new ways for jazz. It's as simple, and as important, as that.

If all of this seems too technical (or boring or whatever) to the reader, let him go to Evans's version of *Young and Foolish*. The piece is in C. Within a half-chorus, Bill is in D flat. And he ends in E. Gracefully, easily, eloquently. The proof of the theory is in the new and unexpected beauties it allows the artist to bring us. And often, and most effectively, without our even noticing.

When Bill Evans first came to jazz piano, Bud Powell was the dominant influence on most younger players, and Powell, whose best recorded work had largely been done by the mid-1950s, was a frustrating influence. Easy to imitate in some aspects by players who knew less about the keyboard than he did, Powell seemed impossible to emulate, and too many of his followers had settled into a kind of middle-register glibness, in which horn-like treble phrases were bounced off of self-accompanying bass lines of "comping" chords. Only Horace Silver had evolved a personal style under Powell's spell, a virtually irresistible one, by reintroducing large doses of blues (i.e., minor thirds) with an assertive swing ("he sounds like Bud imitating Pete Johnson" said one wag at the time).

We heard a lot of very good Powell and some good Silver

on Evans's first record. Try *Our Delight* for Powell; or *Displacement* for Silver; or *No Cover, No Minimum* for both. And we also heard something of the enigmatic, peripheral style of Lennie Tristano. What was not so evident was Evans's professed admiration of Nat Cole as a jazz pianist, evidence of that later became clearer with a change in touch and with Evans's evident commitment to ballads.

I suppose if Bill Evans had done nothing else, he brought some of Tristano's ideas into the mainstream of jazz. But he did much else. To do it, he had to sacrifice some things. The swing that he gave us on *All About Rosie,* and which can be heard virtually throughout his first LP, was a conventional swing, and Evans, to be Evans, had to find his own kind of rhythmic momentum, a momentum integrated with his evolving personal touch and use of dynamics, and his own sense of musical phrase and melodic flow.

I should not leave that first session without pointing out *Five,* Evans's *I Got Rhythm*-based piece whose theme laid out his characteristic interest in rhythmic displacement, with "turning the beat around" on a single short phrase. (If those words don't make the challenge clear, play the opening chorus of *Five* and it will be.)

The twenty-six months that passed between Bill Evans's first and second Riverside LPs were patently fruitful, and what can be heard on the second LP is a remarkable, emerging, Bill Evans style, his influences assimilated (or abandoned), his own approach fully integrated, if not fully developed. And what one hears subsequently is the style's development, and the development of an ensemble style for the Evans Trio. The Powell-like bluntness of touch was gone; the Silver-like blues-iness no longer evident (perhaps because the style came to seem all too easy to be truly expressive for anyone except Horace himself).

The Evans touch—gentle, delicate, always integrated with

perceptive pedal work—had begun to emerge. He seemed, as Miles Davis said, to make a sound rather than strike a chord, but try to decide which notes in any Evans chord were struck forcefully and sustained, and which softly, to achieve those sounds!

Most telling is the musical flow: the flow of ideas one to the next, the magic flow of sound between the hands—the integration of the hands. He was now a pianist discovering the instrument and its resources as he needed them, not a stylist imposing ideas on a keyboard. Returning to the Tristano effect, I find one of the first signs of its assimilation was the way Bill slides into the melody of Harold Arlen's *Come Rain or Come Shine,* teasingly, obliquely, gradually. It was an occasional device which Bill made his own: theme-statements that seem to evolve from improvisation rather than the usual other-way-around. That, and the parallel motion of the two hands on a single phrase. Bill once spoke admiringly of "the way Tristano and Lee Konitz started thinking structurally," and the words suggest that Tristano's horn-playing "students," Konitz and Warne Marsh, affected him as much as did the pianist himself.

Time changes things. It would be foolish to deny that. Even our best and most thoughtful reactions, even our deepest and least transient selves, grow and therefore change. To Evans and the Trio themselves, the "live" Village Vanguard sessions reportedly did not seem so remarkable while they were doing them as they did later in the studio editing sessions, and as they did later still on the LPs. And they no longer seem so uncommunicative to me as they did in 1961. Perhaps I did not properly respond to the rapport among the three men. Still, the Vanguard sessions seem no less introspective to me, yet Evans seems—paradoxically perhaps—no less uncompromisingly exposed emotionally.

I think Bill Evans was the most important and influential white jazz musician after Bix Beiderbecke—and that statement is no reflection on the contribution or the importance of Bunny Berigan, Benny Goodman, Jack Teagarden, Dave Tough, Stan Getz—does Django Reinhardt belong on such a list?—or any other. Partly my statement seems valid to me because of Evans's intrinsic merit, and partly because his effect on the music has been so general—technically, in ways I have commented on, emotionally in its uncompromising lyricism. At the same time I think that in the future, his work may come to seem somewhat isolated from the mainstream—as Bix's now does—but no less valuable and no less authentic and no less beautiful.

Bill Evans's major contribution was, as I say, in an abiding lyricism—again like Beiderbecke's. But such a remark is an observation and a description. It is also perhaps a limitation. But would one *complain* that Lester Young was always playful? Coleman Hawkins dramatic? Or, for that matter, Beethoven humorless?

No, it would be as foolish to deny that lyricism pervades all aspects of Evans's work as to deny the element of privacy in some of it. I can say more about that later quality as I hear it on the previously unissued solo performances that have appeared since Evans's death. They seem to me some of the most private and emotionally naked music I have ever heard. I was shocked at them on first hearing, and if Bill Evans were still with us, I'm not sure I would want to hear them.

But I said above that times changes even our least ephemeral selves. So does death. And *All the Things You Are, Easy To Love, I Loves You Porgy* (a fine sketch for the Montreux masterpiece version on Verve), and the rest now seem to me a heritage invaluable and without precedent in recorded jazz.

There were times when I heard Bill Evans and thought that this music, exposed so unprotected emotionally, so completely naked in its feeling—if you take it into the real world that world will crush it and crush the man who made it.

Perhaps after all that is what happened.

The studio sessions by the classic Evans Trio, with *Falling Leaves* and *Blue in Green* are collected as *"Spring Leaves"* on Milestone M-47034. *Peace Piece* and *Young and Foolish* are included in Milestone 47024. The Village Vangard "live" Trio sessions appear as M-47002. (*Milestones* is among these.) Evans's earliest Riverside date, with *Our Delight, Displacement, Five,* and *No Cover, No Minimum,* is a part of Milestone M-47063.

All About Rosie was last issued on Columbia C2S-831.

(However, as I indicate, this essay appears in much expanded form as a part of the limited edition boxed-set *"The Complete Bill Evans Riverside Recordings."*)

꒜꒜

THIRD STREAM PROBLEMS

In his *Rhapsody in Blue* George Gershwin, according to the phrase of the twenties, "made an honest woman" of jazz. Perhaps he lay down with her and produced a bastard? Or perhaps, since she was an honest woman to begin with, Gershwin only borrowed a few of her jewels?

The *Rhapsody* and Gershwin's other "serious" works are basically European concert music, and a rhythm here, a slur or blue note there—even a twelve-bar blues form—can't really make them jazz. Gershwin was not the first man to indulge in such borrowings, he was merely the first from the "popular" side of the fence. There is reason to believe that European composers were exposed to jazz and its progenitors as long ago as Brahms. (But then there is an eighteenth-century Scarlatti sonata that sounds rather like Meade "Lux" Lewis.)

Gershwin's relationship to jazz—or jazz's to Gershwin—is an intriguing proposition. It is not quite enough to say that his concert works are not really jazz, or to say that his popular songs gave jazzmen some favorite vehicles for their own interpretations and improvisations. *I Got Rhythm* has been deeply inspiring, not only in its harmonic sequence but in its implied rhythmic patterns, to nearly every important jazz musician from Sidney Bechet through Ornette Coleman, and it has become the most durable pattern in the repertory after the twelve-bar blues. Further, anyone who has heard Gershwin the pianist on a piece like his *"I Got Rhythm" Variations* knows that there was more jazz in him than we generally suppose. His contributions would seem far from superficial, but they are rather subtle for a critic or historian to deal with.

It is easy enough to make a list of composers who heard ragtime and jazz early and tried to make some use of it in their work—Debussy, Milhaud, Stravinsky, Ravel, etc. And names like Ives and Copland only begin an American list. Some of the pieces that resulted have been successful, some have not. But in very few cases does the success or lack of it depend on either the authenticity or the extent to which the composer has employed the jazz idiom. One exception might be Ravel's sonata for violin and piano, which attempts to go deeper into jazz than most, and whose middle movement turns out to be a disturbing and unintentional parody of the blues. The most successful early work is probably in Milhaud's *La Création du Monde*. In form, it is pure Euro-

pean classicism; in melody and rhythmic effects it is made
up of the jazzy clichés of the twenties, but nevertheless one
gets the feeling that, of all these composers, Milhaud might
have developed the most authentic grasp of the jazz idiom
had he been interested in pursuing it with discipline. But
he was not. Stravinsky begins with engaging "light" pieces
like the "Piano Rag Music" or sections of *L'Histoire du
Soldat,* but when he writes a more serious work around a
jazz orchestra, he produces the *Ebony Concerto,* which, in
the performances we have heard so far, hardly gives jazz a
telling glance.

Today, almost any American or Western European composer will at least be aware of this vital musical idiom in our
midst. Many are also showing an increasing understanding
of its real qualities and its heritage, and inevitably some of
these men reflect that growing understanding in their own
work. It has become apparent that a casual or superficial reflection of jazz is not enough. Gradually, certain composers
have sought to use the jazz idiom with more commitment—
to use its way of handling sound, its way of phrasing, to use
its musical forms, and most recently even to use jazz improvisation itself. At the same time, certain jazz composers
have looked in the other direction, not merely to borrow
this or that device or practice from Western concert music
and assimilate it into jazz (that is a continuing process, anyway) but to form musical alliances comparable to those the
classicists have undertaken.

Composer Gunther Schuller was the first to speak of such
activities as a "third stream" of music. But his phrase has
since been subject to so much journalistic abuse that it may
well need to be abandoned. There even appeared an LP
called *"Third Stream Jazz"*—rather like an orange tangelo,
I suppose. The first stream was, of course, the Western or
European concert tradition, as it continues in Europe and

as it was long ago transplanted here. The second stream is the continuing evolution of jazz. And the third stream seeks to combine the two, using written forms for classical players, and improvisation by jazzmen, to make *concerto grosso*-like works.

It seems to me natural to ask if some Third Stream composers are attracted to jazz, perhaps unconsciously, because of its ready audience as well as its natural vitality. And it is good to ask if some jazzmen are not attracted to concert music because of false notions of prestige. Some are, in each case, to be sure. But a blanket accusation of opportunism hurled at all the classicists, or of self-defeating delusion hurled at all the jazzmen, would be much too facile. For one thing, it misunderstands a commonplace response of many an artist to his environment. Better to accuse contemporary classicists of hopeless effeteness if some of them did not respond, and respond deeply, to jazz. And after all, any opportunism involved will reveal itself in an opportunistic and shallow music that results. To sniff suspiciously around *all* Third Stream efforts on principle is perhaps to find an easy way to avoid real appreciation or evaluation of the results.

The problems in Third Stream music are complex, even if some of them are fairly obvious. One work, evidently inspired by obvious analogies of early jazz to Bach and Handel, pits a more or less "Dixieland" style *concertanti* of players against an *orchestra*. But in performance, the Dixieland men are simply drawn from the symphonic ranks, and their phrasing will be frequently stiff and occasionally ludicrous. Also, the ability of such men to indulge in a real improvisation may turn out to be almost nil. Only experienced jazzmen can play jazz. And nowadays few classical players—except church organists—can improvise well in any idiom.

A somewhat more intriguing work, which received a great

deal of attention a few years ago, is Swiss composer Rolf Liebermann's *Concerto for Jazz Band and Orchestra,* which juxtaposes a big jazz band and a symphony orchestra, again in *concerto grosso* style. Liebermann did not ask for improvising; still that would not really prevent the jazz involved from being jazz. But Liebermann's concept of jazz then seemed almost a hold-over from the twenties: the term seemed to mean almost any North American (or even South American) popular music. Further, his knowledge of these idioms seemed to have its gaps to say the least: a section marked "boogie woogie," for instance, has little or nothing to do with boogie woogie. Also, it was rather painfully obvious that Stan Kenton is very much to Liebermann's taste. But Liebermann's final section, marked "mambo," is undeniably a crowd-rouser, and a diverting one.

A piece by Gunther Schuller called *Transformation* shows much more awareness of the problems involved in Third Stream music—problems not only of phrasing but, at last, of using real improvisation. Schuller is well equipped to deal with them. He is primarily a classical player and composer whose knowledge of jazz is not only sympathetic but historically authentic and penetrating—"knowledge" is not the right word: let's call it love.

Transformation begins with a small classical orchestra in Schuller's contemporary compositional idiom. A jazz group makes itself known, at first complementing the classical lines. But gradually the jazzmen begin to coax the classicists over to their way of phrasing. Soon the piece is completely transformed as the jazzmen begin to improvise on the blues. After a bit, the classical players return, reverse things into their style again, and it is largely they who finish off the performance. (Incidentally, the recorded version of this work is especially graced by the improvising of pianist Bill Evans.) There may be something a bit too polite, too self-effacing, in using such a mutual deference of each idiom for the other. But *Transformation* was a firm step.

Subsequently, there were some other steps that seemed backward, or at least sideways. Leonard Bernstein and the New York Philharmonic premiered a rather pretentious and aridly "experimental" piece by Teo Macero for jazz group and orchestra. Under the same auspices, there was performed Howard Brubeck's *Dialogues for Jazz Combo and Orchestra*—an example of bad conservative classical writing, with sometimes genially *ersatz* jazz from Howard's brother Dave.*

Firm steps forward were again taken at a 1959 Town Hall concert, jointly performed by the Modern Jazz Quartet and the 1959 Beaux Arts String Quartet. Each group offered pieces from its own repertory, and the two groups joined for John Lewis's *Sketch* and Gunther Schuller's *Conversation*.

Lewis's brief piece is perhaps even less than a sketch. In a sense, it is a curious little Haydn pastiche, built around a single descending phrase which is handled with some ingenuity by each group of players in its own idiom. But at the same time, the piece meets the Third Stream composer's major problem directly. For Lewis made no effort to get the classical players to use jazz phrasing, an especially difficult proposition with string players. Nor did he ask the members of the MJQ (as he has done in some of his jazz pieces!) to deport themselves like classicists.

Gunther Schuller's *Conversation* used the same principle, but took it further. And instead of trying to ally the idioms gradually as in *Transformation,* Schuller let each assert itself fully. In outline (and with some simplification), the string quartet begins *Conversation* in Schuller's contempo-

---

* I am inclined to except Bernstein's later performance of Larry Austin's piece *Improvisations for Jazz Soloists and Orchestra* from such censure, however.

rary atonal idiom, but with some percussive and harmonic complements from members of the jazz group. (How could one add anything effective to so delicately balanced a medium as the string quartet? Schuller did.) When the strings have built a deadlock of tension, the jazz players arrive almost abruptly, relieving it with easy, tonal improvisation. As the jazzmen build their own kind of tension, the strings reenter beneath them. And a debate ensues. The piece concludes on a somewhat John Lewis-like resolution—a respectful agreement to disagree.

It has been said that it is incongruous to hear a jazz bass player suddenly begin walking quarter-notes after some twentieth-century atonality. But that is precisely the point of this piece, precisely its structural premise. The tension between these two idioms, with each allowed to express itself fully, even competitively, is what makes *Conversation* work. And such a structure is in almost complete contrast to the kind of deferences between the groups of players that Schuller used in *Transformation*.

Schuller has done one other Third Stream piece that was initially conceived for the Modern Jazz Quartet, this time with a full orchestra, a strangely Gershwinesque *Concertino for Jazz Quartet and Orchestra*. The score does raise the problem of getting at least a few of the symphony men to swing and use jazz phrasing. But it throws far more difficult tasks at the jazzman: meters they are not used to, unfamiliar forms (a thirteen-bar blues—why?), and the task of deliberately accelerating their tempo. Under the circumstances, it would seem almost impossible to get a comfortable and relaxed performance of the *Concertino*.

In *Abstraction* Schuller took still another approach. The piece is a brief serial composition, in mirror form (the second part is an exact reversal of the first), for augmented string quartet. It was originally conceived for Ornette Coleman, who improvised against its first and second parts and invented a cadenza between them. The idiom is predominantly classical, but Coleman is asked to play his responses to it in his own way. In the recorded version he darts in and out, sometimes playing with the strings, sometimes against them, but the performance is an emotional whole.

Schuller has also written two sets of "variants" on established jazz compositions, one on John Lewis's *Django,* the other on Thelonious Monk's *Criss Cross.* The former is perhaps not quite so successful in conception, or in execution on the recorded version. There are some rather surging and turbulent moments, both written and improvised, that will seem out of place to some people in a lyric work like *Django.* But it seems to me that the implications are there in Lewis's piece, for there is more to *Django,* in any performance, than lyricism. One problem in the *Django* variants is the viola solo that introduces the second part: I have heard it several times and it always comes out as Viennese schmaltz—quite a contrast to the lovely way Jim Hall's guitar opens the first section on some of the same thematic material.

The *Variants on a Theme of Thelonious Monk,* on Monk's *Criss Cross,* is on an already major Monk piece, indeed one of the major compositions in the jazz repertory. And except perhaps for one slow interlude (the second variant), Schuller has actually produced a brilliant jazz arrangement, which owes little or nothing to classicism except for forms and skills that Schuller has assimilated in his own experience as a composer. The improvising in the first section is especially intriguing, being done in a kind of relay form with each soloist momentarily overlapping the previous player in sometimes simultaneous invention. On the recording, the juxtaposition of Ornette Coleman and Eric Dolphy, and the differences in the way they phrase, is tellingly dra-

matic, as is the Monkish understanding Coleman uses in rephrasing the theme itself, early in his solo.

In a sense we have come full circle here, with the Monk
Variants as a jazz arrangement, on a major jazz piece, done
by a classical and Third Stream composer. Beside this, the
current efforts of classicist Lukas Foss to get his players to
improvise in their own idiom is perhaps only the other side
of the coin.

Two recordings, one written by an important jazz player
and writer, the other by a well known composer-arranger,
attracted a great deal of attention when they were first issued. Both are more or less in the Third Stream idiom. The
first is J. J. Johnson's *Perceptions,* written for Dizzy Gillespie. The piece shows increasing orchestral subtlety and
skill on the part of the composer, and it must have delighted
the musicians who played it. To others, it may seem only a
succession of perhaps commendable effects. In either case, it
seems to me that one problem is that it was not really written *for* Gillespie, or perhaps anyone like him, for it asks him
to execute written parts of a sort that are hardly his wont.
And in only a couple of places does *Perceptions* call on him
to do what he does best—open up and play!—and those moments are a joy.

The other work is Eddie Sauter's *Focus,* a skillful but occasionally derivative string work (derivative of Bartók),
against which Stan Getz improvised. *Focus* is a rolling tour
de force for Getz, but Sauter offered a sort of advanced
David Rose writing with some of the schmaltz drained off.
At any rate, the juxtaposition of Getz and the orchestra
never seems to cut very deep.

An LP recital called *"An Image"* was written by Bill
Russo around Lee Konitz. Konitz improvised with a string
group augmented by a few jazz players, and some of the
pieces are in a classical idiom. Russo has also on occasion

arrived at a provocative use of strings in jazz by having them
play with minimum vibrato and supplementing them with a
guitar.

Two other recent pieces dramatize the current problems
of the Third Stream. *Around the Blues* by André Hodeir is
perhaps not really a Third Stream work, but it surrounds
several choruses of Milt Jackson's blues playing with orchestral sections, with plaintive flutes predominating. The piece
leans heavily on Jackson. In the end we may feel that basically we have what we had already: Milt and the blues. (Perhaps if Hodeir the composer of the *Jazz Cantata* could work
with a major jazz improviser?) German composer Werner
Heider's appropriately titled *Divertimento* (it is a diversion
at best, I would say) alternates statements by the orchestra
and statements by the Modern Jazz Quartet effectively, each
in its own idiom, but Heider's writing seems less commendable. But it is a joy to hear the Quartet executing its sudden
entrances with such immediate swing.

I have heard Mercer Ellington and a group of highly spirited (although otherwise not particularly notable) jazz players encourage the late members of the Beaux Arts Quartet
into a momentary swing (the group reorganized in about
1960). But in a sense the problem rests where it is left by
Conversation, Abstraction, and the *Monk Variants:* one can
still find only a few classical players who can phrase in the
jazz idiom, and one can find only a few technically skilled
jazz players with an interest in undertaking more complex
written classical parts.

Are we deadlocked for the moment at the point where
Third Stream pieces *must* let the two idioms argue and
even battle? At the point where few classicists will truly understand the jazz idiom and few jazzmen the classical? But
where at least one or two jazzmen can improvise well, even
within classical structures? Perhaps. And perhaps that is all

we should wish for or expect. It is conceivable that the
Third Stream is not a stream but actually an eddy, but I do
not think it likely.

As I say, we have had some few successful pieces—*works*
quite beyond the status of "efforts" or "experiments." But
there are several signs that the future will be different. A recent concert piece by a young composer, David Reck, contains a part for tenor saxophone—a rare event in itself, but
the part is marked to be played with a tone like Ornette
Coleman's, and the writing shows considerable knowledge
of Coleman's work. Further, the piece contains a few brief
spaces in which the players—whoever they are and whatever
their background—are asked to improvise. And the beautifully shimmering ending can be extended ad lib, the players
being cued according to the conductor's discretion and feeling for the moment.

Yes, the future will be different.   (*1963*)

ALBERT AYLER, FOR EXAMPLE

A few months ago, in reviewing an LP by the young soprano
and tenor saxophonist Albert Ayler in this space, I said that
Ayler might be working out a perfectly valid musical language of his own, but that it perhaps might be best not to
intrude until he has things further along. More recent releases by Ayler make me realize that if such a view does not
need to be altogether abandoned, it does need to be drasti-
cally reconsidered.

A new Fantasy LP called *"My Name Is Albert Ayler"*
(Fantasy 6016; stereo 86016) is a recital of only limited suc-

cess. But paradoxically it is at the same time a highly enlightening one, and not only about Ayler's talents but about
the intentions of the jazz *avant-garde* in general. The LP is
an American release of music recorded in Denmark a couple
of years ago. The repertory is, on the face of it, conventional,
and includes readings of *Bye Bye Blackbird, Summertime,
On Green Dolphin Street,* and the blues by Charlie Parker
called *Billie's Bounce.* Besides Ayler, the ensemble includes
two Danish musicians, on piano and bass, and a young
American drummer. The pianist, particularly, is thoroughly
capable and (like hundreds of pianists the world over) thoroughly schooled in the conventions of bebop or modern
jazz; he is also (again like hundreds of pianists) bland, slick,
almost thoroughly dull, and to Ayler, apparently, almost
thoroughly inhibiting. At first impression, Ayler's playing
declares above all else: let me be free of this thoroughly capable, slick, bland, dull, conventional music.

Does Albert Ayler attempt to make music only from a
negative premise, then? Well, perhaps that is only one's first
impression.

One's second impression is apt to be even more negative,
however. Out of Ayler's saxophone come notes that are over-
blown, honked, twisted, growled, shrieked. Indeed, he sometimes sounds like an amateur who simply has not learned
the proper embouchure for a reed instrument or the proper
fingering for the saxophone. Yet at other times he perfectly
articulates strings of difficult, short notes, fleet runs, and perfectly pronounced saxophone tones. It is evident that Albert
Ayler is a very good saxophonist indeed. And putting one
and one together, it is therefore necessarily evident that
whatever Ayler plays on his instrument, he plays deliberately. Ayler has decided that whatever sound he can cause
his horn to make, that sound might become a part of his
music. Much as King Oliver decided that the wail produced

by putting a pop bottle in the bell of his cornet was a part
of his music, and much as Sidney Bechet decided that the
growl produced partly in his throat was a part of his music,
and much as Rex Stewart decided that the choked sound
produced by pushing the cornet valve only halfway down
was a part of his music, so Albert Ayler has decided that the
honk or whinny produced by a too-slack use of the saxophone reed can be a part of his music.

Ayler plays the melodies of *Bye Bye Blackbird* and *Billie's
Bounce* with a kind of antiswing and calculated carelessness—almost as though he did not quite know them or know
how to play them. And he approaches the slower ballads,
Summertime and *On Green Dolphin Street,* with what seems
at first a deliberate bathos. Does deliberate bathos make for
parody? I think not, but I do think that in Ayler's music a
kind of bizarre beauty emerges.

Much contemporary art has as a major purpose the deliberate esthetic exposure and destruction of old standards.
That is a quality shared, it seems to me, by Picasso, Joyce,
the Marx Brothers, and the Three Stooges, as well as earlier
jazz. And I believe that with much truly contemporary art
one also sees the emergence, however tentative, of new standards. All well and good, but a work may be fully contemporary in tone and still not be very good. The Marx Brothers were superb comedians but the Three Stooges were not.

The test of Ayler's music comes when he is not boxed in
by conventional standards and conventional formats. On
C.T., he is accompanied only by the superb young Danish
bassist Niels-Henning Petersen and the very good drummer
Ronnie Gardiner, and he is allowed to roam freely. I appreciate the challenge involved; I appreciate the careful and
attentive response of the accompanists; I appreciate the passion and the daring of Ayler's improvisation. But I would
be less than honest if I were to deny that after a few minutes

of the performance I was no longer engaged; I felt, as I often feel with John Coltrane, that I had attended a search of twelve minutes' duration for a reward of three.

A later Ayler can be heard on a record I have mentioned in this space before, ESP-Disc 1002, with the perhaps regrettably portentous title of *"Spiritual Unity."* Here, with a trio, Ayler explores four thematically related pieces, all built on simple (and, for me, simplistic) compositional ideas. Ayler's solos are frequently orderly and logical developments, especially so on a piece called *The Wizard*—more orderly than many of John Coltrane's but, for me, less imaginative than Ornette Coleman's.

The most recent of Ayler's recordings is something of a reversal. It is a one-sided LP of a single work called *Bells* (ESP-Disc 1010), recorded by a sextet during a concert. The opening portion features some simultaneous improvisation by all the horns, and is perhaps deliberately anarchic. This is followed by a cadenza by Ayler; it is teasingly effective but it prepares us for nothing more daring than music built around simple marchlike themes, featuring an ordinary triad and performed with more than an echo of the shakily intoned, archetypal brass bands of New Orleans!

Any conclusions I would have to offer on Ayler at this point are necessarily tentative; I would say that as a composer he has a sense of form superior to his sense of melody, and that as an improviser he gains stature among players of "the new thing" from that same sense of form.   (*1965*) ỡ❧

TALKING WITH MYSELF
(with limited apologies
to Edmund Wilson)

Visitor: You have written several times about the so-called "new thing." Would you describe yourself as one of its partisans?

Williams: Well, let's say that I like many things about it, that I think those things are inevitable and most welcome. Also that I think that Ornette Coleman's is a major talent. The term is unfortunate, not just because it is awkward—is "new thing" any more awkward than bebop?—but because there are several approaches at the moment being called "new thing" or "free form jazz."

Visitor: What things about it are inevitable and welcome?

Williams: Well, for one, the fact that I don't need eight bars to make a variation on a musical idea that it takes me eight bars to state. That I don't have to keep repeating the basic structure of a piece exactly. That should be obvious—it is in other musics—but only recently has jazz really taken advantage of it. Then, second, there is what is happening to rhythm sections. The bass is becoming a more melodic, less purely percussive and harmonic instrument. The bass can now do something besides just, shall we say, "accompany" other players and take an occasional solo. Mingus showed the way to this several years ago. And drums, if they are used, can also play musical phrases in an almost contrapuntal part, with less time-keeping. With some exceptions much modern drumming has been so conservative since, say, the Max Roach of 1947—it even became reac-

83

tionary, and for a while took a step backward. Then Roy Haynes beautifully reasserted the modern style and Elvin Jones and others took off from it. Basically, I'd say that the idea in the new thing is that jazz improvising can be done another way than by just following a bass line, a chordal outline, over and over and over again. Recently, groups have also shown remarkable abilities at spontaneous, collective changes of tempo—again, Mingus pointed the way here. It is a similar question, actually: why should variations all be at the same tempo?

Visitor: What about the business of unusual time signatures in some current jazz, 5/8 . . . that sort of thing?

Williams: It is rather awkwardly done sometimes, isn't it? Actually new-thing music is far beyond that. Monk long ago pointed to freer metres, and to the young players, metres are often so free that each melodic phrase might call for its own time signature.

Visitor: Well, of course, the usual word from the opposition is that the horn men lack order, discipline, or pattern in their solos.

Williams: I know, and I find this very curious. The obvious question would be: what sort of order and discipline do these people hear in most jazz improvising? Where is the discipline when one does follow the harmonic outline of a pop song or the blues? For a just average player, there may be none, really. He follows a chorus which repeats over and over and which, for an AABA song form, has internal repeats as well. Then his order is automatic, I suppose. Well, what has this to do with discipline? Not very much, actually. Suppose our player memorizes a lot of licks, learns them in different keys, and learns how the licks fit different chords. Then, when he solos, he strings them together. Such playing would have nothing to do with order. And there is a lot of it going on.

Visitor: But is that what the *best* soloists do? Soloists before the new thing, I mean.

Williams: Oh no. Besides their originality and their willingness to take real chances with their melodic ideas, the best soloists improvise with melodic order, not just the more or less automatic harmonic order that comes from running the chords. A solo like Parker's *Embraceable You,* or *Lady Be Good,* a good Miles Davis blues solo, Monk on *Bags' Groove*—these are a few examples—I'm just pulling them out at random, there are many hundreds of other examples one might use—of great solos built on linking, sequential melodic ideas. Parker's *Embraceable,* for example, is built around an elaboration of his opening phrase. He plays it five times at the beginning and in various ingenious permutations throughout. Same way with Monk on *Bags' Groove.* These soloists don't lean on merely running chords. They make orderly melodies—in this way or in various other ways. Even if we don't hear such order exactly, I think we sense it.

Visitor: You don't mean to tell me you hear this sort of thing in Ornette Coleman?

Williams: I sure do! *Just* this sort of thing. Which is why I brought up the subject of that kind of sequential order. As I also indicated, I needn't have drawn my examples from the modernists only. King Oliver's solos are built on sequential ideas. So are Teddy Wilson's—and all the great players.

Visitor: Well, can you give some examples from Coleman's records?

Williams: Have you ever heard Ornette's piece called *C & D?* The written melody develops logically from the opening idea, and the writing there is an excellent introduction to his playing. But of course writing is done at leisure and playing is done spontaneously. So we'd better turn to his improvising. I think a good introduction to Ornette's sense of order in his solos is his work on the first part of the

"Variants" on Monk's *Criss Cross* he did with Gunther
Schuller. Ornette develops Monk's melody itself. Not that
he just *plays* the melody. He gets inside it and makes striking variations on it—in a manner that I think might please
Monk very much, by the way. It takes a rare and exacting
sense of musical discipline to do this sort of thing, you know.
On that piece Eric Dolphy follows Ornette. Dolphy is a very
good player indeed, but his solo there does not have the
kind of cohesion Coleman's does. Or take a longer solo.
Have you ever listened closely to *Congeniality?* Ornette's
variations are based on about five related musical ideas.
The same sort of order happens on his *R.P.D.D.* Those are
just three examples.

Visitor: I was warned that you often get technical!

Williams: Look, I know some people feel a sense of hor-
ror at such a discussion of music. But when musicians like
Ornette Coleman are being accused of a lack of discipline
and of inviting chaos, there is nothing to do but point out
the order and the discipline in their work. Anyway, we
aren't really getting technical. All I'm saying is, listen to
melody as melody, and most people do that anyway. Incidentally, we might notice that the people who call the new
thing undisciplined are often the same people who profess
to abhor any discussion of music as music. Anyway, I have
no business getting *technical*—I'd make too many mistakes.

Visitor: What about Coleman's intonation?

Williams: I have said my say on this before. In the first
place, what is called good intonation (put that *good* in
quotes) is perhaps a convention of European music. Its standards do not apply to other musics. Most men by nature
apparently sing or play in curves of melody, not in a series
of true pitches (put that *true* in quotes too). In any case, it
is still possible to talk about Coleman and the others in
terms of the European tradition and the jazz tradition—

both. It's been said that Ornette uses the pitch of the alto sax as it is, rather than the pitch of the piano. That is, that he makes frank use of the fact that when the middle range of the alto is in tune, the top and bottom of the instrument will be a little off. That may be, but my own feeling is that basically Ornette extends the idea of the blue notes—or rather that he takes it back to where it was originally with the older blues singers. Instead of bluecing or bending an occasional note, Coleman will inflect a whole melodic line, a whole passage, for emotional effect. But if you listen carefully, I think you will hear enough key notes of phrases that are on pitch to let you know that Ornette is quite aware, intuitively and probably literally, of what he is doing.

Visitor: So far you seem to have been talking mostly about Ornette Coleman. What about other horn men?

Williams: Well, I have also mentioned Eric Dolphy respectfully. However, I confess it sometimes seems to me that Dolphy is a bit more comfortable when he plays with the chord changes, or at least the outline of a piece, directly in mind, than when he is improvising modally or more freely. Dolphy is probably somewhere between John Coltrane and Ornette, roughly speaking. Of course recently Coltrane has followed Ornette into a freer improvising without either chord changes or four- and eight-bar phrases in mind.

Visitor: Well, that's only three men. Come now.

Williams: Frankly, I think there are some fakers aspiring to the new thing. Yes, I mean fakers, who have little idea what they are doing. You might think that such a free music invites faking. That's true, but let's not forget that there were fake beboppers in the early days of modern jazz—and some fake jazzmen in all periods.

Visitor: Well then, those who aren't faking?

Williams: I have long respected Cecil Taylor—that should go without saying. There is certainly nothing fake about

Paul Bley. There is Sonny Simmons, who is to Ornette as
Sonny Stitt was to Charlie Parker, or as Jabbo Smith used to
be to Louis Armstrong—Simmons has learned his Coleman.
Incidentally, let's not forget the older players who are coming to terms with the new thing. I confess I find Sonny
Rollins's efforts so far a little unconvincing, but perhaps
that is because I have so great a respect for the kind of
larger, let us call it orchestral, form—even beyond good soloist's form—that Rollins has shown. Incidentally, I have heard
Coleman go on for too long. Then there is Jackie McLean's
recent shift into freer improvising. McLean's move should
not surprise, by the way. When I first heard Ornette, I was
reminded of Jackie McLean's tone and of his efforts to
break up Charlie Parker's rhythms. Most important, there
is that Miles Davis album called *"Kind of Blue,"* where the
musicians played from scales rather than chords—"modal"
playing, it's usually called. Many, many have followed that
idea. Dexter Gordon has even done some so-called modal
improvising—that is, for our purposes, making up his melodies from a series of assigned notes rather than to fit a series
of assigned chords. Anyway, George Russell fairly long ago
asked soloists to improvise without chord changes—and don't
forget the beautiful way Bill Evans responded on *All About
Rosie.* That was several years before George formed his new
thing sextet.

Visitor: You've mentioned Mingus.

Williams: Yes, and I should have. There's more. Mingus
tried so-called free improvising on records quite a while
back in things like *Gregorian Chant.* And give credit to
Lennie Tristano and his associates for the unpremeditated
improvising of *Intuition.*

Visitor: Still others?

Williams: What about the bass players! Charlie Haden,
the late Scott LaFaro, Steve Swallow, Gary Peacock, Ron

Carter. Have you heard Richard Davis, as they say, play free? Look, there are a lot more good players than there is any point in our just *naming*.

Visitor: You haven't said much about John Coltrane.

Williams: Because his current approach to free improvising seems very different to me from, say, Ornette's. It seems incantive, and almost a matter of emotional endurance. I don't hear Coleman's specifically musical development of key ideas, for instance.

Visitor: You're not saying that everyone should play the new thing?

Williams: Oh, no! Or, anyway it depends entirely on the player. Would anybody in his right mind want Ben Webster to change? But I think everybody has to come to terms with it in some sense—if only to accept the fact that it is here and very vital, and is capturing many of the more talented young players. Actually, it might not *hurt* almost any player to try it. He might find out, as Pee Wee Russell and Jimmy Giuffre have, that playing this way doesn't actually change him so much as it lets him be himself more than ever, and Giuffre has developed a wonderful sense of musical ellipsis.

Visitor: Anything else?

Williams: Yes. It has to do with the theme-and-variations idea. Even the terms are bad because they imply that the variations are secondary, whereas in small-group jazz they are the music for the most part. In conventional modern jazz, the theme stops abruptly after the opening chorus, having set up some chords. Even when the players don't blow on chords, the transition from theme to improvising is often just as abrupt. Of course, a player can use the melody itself in his improvising in ingenious ways—and I'm not just talking about old timers, listen to Monk or to Ornette, as I was saying earlier. But there are more ingenious and provocative solutions in some of Mingus's pieces and some of Cecil Taylor's. The theme seems to emerge from a kind of collective, semi-improvised opening. Once gradually arrived at, it is stated as a sort of agreed-upon musical *matter* and point of departure for the soloist. This matter gradually retreats as one player takes over for his variations. At the end, it will gradually re-emerge for a closing statement. The piece Taylor calls *Bulbs* is a good example.

Visitor: I suppose I should do some listening at this point.

Williams: Feel free. The records are right there, against the wall. But you'll have to do your own browsing.

The visitor browsed and noted the following:

The *Variants on a Theme of Thelonious Monk* with Ornette Coleman and Eric Dolphy is on Atlantic 1365. Both Dolphy and Coleman are also on Coleman's *"Free Jazz"* on Atlantic 1364. *Congeniality* is on Atlantic 1317, and *R.P.D.D.* on Atlantic 1378.

Cecil Taylor's work can be heard on Contemporary 3562 (*"Looking Ahead"*) and his *Bulbs* on Impulse A-30 (under Gil Evans's name, oddly). Sonny Simmons is on Contemporary M3610 (*"Cry!"*) and Impulse A-49.

The Jimmy Giuffre Three with Paul Bley and Steve Swallow are on Verve 8402.

Jackie McLean's *"Let Freedom Ring"* is Blue Note 4106. The best introduction to the George Russell sextet is probably Riverside 341.

ह~

FOUR SAXOPHONISTS

The World Saxophone Quartet is the most important thing
to happen in jazz in over a decade. Now *there's* a statement
that needs further comment.

The group is basically David Murray on tenor, Hamiet
Bluiett on baritone, Oliver Lake and Julius Hempill on
altos. But they all double—and even triple—on an array of
saxes, flutes, and clarinets.

One of the most exciting things about them is what they've
done with the rhythm section. The jazz rhythm section has
been in a state of flux since the string bass replaced the tuba.
More recently, one group drops the piano, another the drums
as well (but puts back the long-departed rhythm guitar), and
bassists and drummers do less time-keeping and play more
musical phrases. Yet we still have a music in which two
horns are accompanied by the same three instruments who
support a sixteen-piece band.

The World Saxophone Quartet's solution is singular:
they have no rhythm section. But they move and swing with
a compelling ease. In its way, the development is very much
like the arrival of the string quartet in European music, and
just about as full of promise.

One great recent master of the string quartet was of course
Bartók and there's quite a Bartók influence in the World
Saxophone Quartet's music. That means that some people
are going to find the WSQ's music "strident." If they do
they're going to be missing the Quartet's musical humor,
and that's rather like missing the expansive humor of Louis
Armstrong or the sardonic wit of Thelonious Monk which
preceded them.

Still, there's the expected seriousness in the WSQ's members as well. David Murray has explored his horn to the extent of finding and using several notes on the top of the tenor sax that nobody knew were there before. He has also mastered saxophone "chords," the simultaneous sounding of two notes on the horn. Both Murray and Lake perform and make records on their own as well, and if Sonny Rollins could be said to have a successor on tenor saxophone, it's David Murray.

The Quartet is an enthralling experience in person, spread across a stage, collectively improvising in a kind of contemporary projection of New Orleans style, with a clarity and sureness almost too good to believe. And that sureness brings up another WSQ accomplishment. In some of their best pieces, we just aren't aware of what is composed, what is pre-arranged, and what is made up on the spot. That all-of-a-piece quality is something jazzmen have been reaching for over a generation. With the Quartet, whole performances sound extemporized.

As I say, there's nothing quite like hearing them "live." But they have some really good records. The best place to start with the World Saxophone Quartet is the LP called *"Steppin'"* on Black Saint BSR 0027, particularly the title piece. Also, don't miss *R&B*, where (wisely) the producers declined to edit out an exhilarating conversation on the excitement of what they've just played, and on what kind of ending to tape-edit onto it.

Black Saint, by the way, is an Italian label, and the World Saxophone Quartet has also recorded for Moers Music, a German label. Getting our cars from Germans, Italians, and Japanese is one thing, but the fact is that they've recently recorded some of our most significant music. Anyway, don't miss the World Saxophone Quartet on Black Saint. And don't miss them live. *(1984)*

᠍᠍᠍᠍᠍

JUST ASKING

I have some questions—or rather I have one question which I'll put in at least two ways. I don't pretend I know the answer. But I have a feeling that anyone who does will have a greater insight into the psyche of mankind in the twentieth century than he could gain any other way. So surely the question is worth asking.

Putting it in terms of my generation: why would it be that a young man growing up in Chicago in the teens of this century, the son of Russian Jewish immigrant parents, would want to learn to play the clarinet like a colored Creole from New Orleans named Jimmy Noone? Why would the act of doing that be so meaningful to him? And having done that, why would he then want to form an orchestra that played like that of an American mulatto from Georgia named Fletcher Henderson? And stake his career in music on doing that? And after he had done that, why would the world make him a celebrity and one of the most famous musicians of the century?

I write of course of Benny Goodman.

Let me put essentially the same question in terms of a later generation. Why would it be that a skinny kid from London, an economics student, would want to try to sing like a relatively ignorant black man from Mississippi? Why would that be so meaningful to him? And having done that as best he could, why would the world make him a star, a sex symbol, and a millionaire? And why would audiences want to watch him sing on stages in huge auditoriums in a lamé jumpsuit with on occasion (I'm told) a padded cod piece?

I write of course of Mick Jagger.

93

So there won't be any misunderstanding, let me be specific about something that I've merely hinted at: I have respect for what Benny Goodman did. In the first place, he became a better clarinetist than Jimmy Noone, and even a better jazz clarinetist, if you will: he had more swing, and showed better basic knowledge of harmony in his improvising. Furthermore, it seems qiute wrong to me to say that Goodman was exploiting Henderson's music (or Jimmy Mundy's music or Edgar Sampson's music). He was playing it and conducting it with dedication and responsibility—and more precision and technical care than Henderson's own orchestra played it. Goodman was playing some of the best American music he could find the best way he knew how. (He also, early on, brought off the miracle of having a white band whose brass and reeds could play with a relaxed swing in 1936 while its rhythm section couldn't!)

If I do not hear the *depth* in Goodman's versions of *Wrappin' It Up* or *Down South Camp Meeting* that I do in Henderson's originals, do not hear the inner strength in Goodman's *Madhouse* that I hear in Earl Hines's version, then I should confess such reactions. But I could not thereby accuse Goodman of deliberately popularizing or debasing the music.

Mick Jagger seems to me another matter. Musically and technically, the challenge he undertook was a considerably lesser one to be sure, and culturally surely a more puzzling one. The integrity with which Jagger approached the challenge may have been comparable to Goodman's in the beginning. But a thinly veiled, insidious exploitation of sexuality, drugs, sadomasochism, and, more recently, sexism soon took over his career.

In any case, Jagger's act does not seem to me very interesting musically. More important, like that of many another rocker, American and British, his strikes me as a really offensive blackface act. No, clearly one does not need makeup to do musical blackface. And if that quality was and is unconscious on Jagger's part, it is perhaps all the more reprehensible in this day and age.

I hasten to add that I have not felt that way about white jazz musicians, not felt they were doing an exploitive burlesque (unintentional burlesque) of a black man's art. Oh, the original Dixieland Jazz Band's recordings make me feel uncomfortable in their shallowness, to be sure. And Woody Herman's singing has given me similar reservations. But not the dedication Herman's clarinet shows to Barney Bigard; not the tribute his alto makes to Johnny Hodges; nor the sound seriousness of Herman's career as leader of a jazz orchestra. And Jack Teagarden always seemed to me to carry the "blackness" in his music as easily as he held his horn.

Of course there is the question of why mass audiences seemed to want to hear Goodman over Henderson and Jagger over Muddy Waters. But it can't be blamed on Goodman that more people wanted to hear him than wanted to hear Chick Webb, or on Jagger that more people attended him than John Lee Hooker.

My question here is what drew Benny and Mick to make such a music in the first place, and such large audiences to want to hear it at all? Both men obviously express something deeply, abidingly important for their followers. What is it?

Why do we all, at whatever level, find such meaning in the musical culture of Afro-Americans? Why has their music so triumphed throughout the world? We invoke it to get through our adolescence and most of us then keep it, one way or another, central in our lives.

As I say, I can't answer my question but if I could, I think I'd know more about what we are and what we might become than any man alive. (*1984*)

II
Musicians at Work

REHEARSING WITH ORNETTE

Ornette Coleman was holding a rehearsal in a room at the new Atlantic Records studios off Columbus Circle. (It was in a recording studio on Columbus Circle that Fletcher Henderson met Don Redman in the early twenties!) Past the double doors of the soundproofed rehearsal room were Coleman, his new trumpeter, Bobby Bradford; Charles "C.M." Moffett, the stocky drummer Bradford had recommended and brought along with him from Texas; and bassist Jimmy Garrison. There was also the group's manager, Mildred Fields (on the telephone, of course); and a couple of visitors were in and out briefly. In a corner of the room—quiet, constantly listening, but with the expression on his face as relaxed as the rest of him—was John Coltrane, and of all the people interested in Coleman's music Coltrane has become one of the most interested. The room was small but there was no feeling of confinement. There was a piano against one wall, and Ornette Coleman used it from time to time to make points, but used it sparingly.

The group had finished running through the ensemble of a new piece as written out on a slip of manuscript paper. Coleman, sitting at the piano, said over his shoulder to Jimmy Garrison, "I'm going to write out the bass line on this one. Use these notes on the piece, but don't make it sound like one note going into the other."

"Can I do that without using the bow?" asked Garrison.

"*Can* you? That's what I'm asking!" They both laughed. Ornette turned to the group. "This time just play the melody for the *emotion*. Just play it as quarter notes for the emotion." They ran through the theme again, phrasing it strangely while concentrating on feeling. At the end, Coleman said quickly, "Okay—let's try it a little faster," as he sat down on the piano bench, playing his alto at the back of the group.

At the end of another try, Coleman suddenly turned to Garrison. "Yeah! You dig that? You almost did it! Play that same thought out. Don't play it like bass notes—don't get that kind of sound like you're walking behind someone. This is a musical phrase." Then he played the bass line on his saxophone, after a false start. "Don't read it as a *time* phrase."

They were now into the piece again with bassist Garrison now beginning to make a complex pattern of rhythms instead of accompanying as the group went into the final part of the tune. When they finished, Coleman turned to Moffett. "Can you make a five stroke roll under him at the end of that phrase, at the same time he is doing that?" As Moffett consented he turned again to the whole group, "Then we go into the playing," smiling, "I mean the . . . uumm . . . improvising."

Garrison: "I'll find out how many different notes I can play against that E that you guys hold at the end of the ensemble."

Coleman: "Yes! That's it, that's it!" They did the number again, with brief solos from Coleman and Bobby Bradford. At the end, the leader again turned to the bassist. "You know," he said as if he had just realized it himself (perhaps he had), "you can go down in fourths behind us on that piece if you want to." Then to the room in general, "I can't find the tempo to make the notes sound right on this one," running over the theme on his alto at a new speed.

The occasion had certainly taken on a character of its own—perhaps a revealing one about Ornette Coleman's music. There was discussion of techniques, and there was technical language being used (some of it conventional, some of it almost homemade), but the meaning behind the language was usually quite evident. And it was not the sort of discussion one would ordinarily hear at a rehearsal—not all of it, anyway. Complex and subtle things—points of phrasing a melody and unison playing—were simply understood and executed without a thought. During the whole afternoon, for instance, no one ever signaled a tempo or even gave an obvious downbeat! Yet everyone started together and stayed together. But some comparatively simple things had to be emphasized—you *can* play descending fourths on this piece, although in this music some other basic practices of tonality might not work; an unaccented five-stroke drum roll might be phrased slightly differently; forget the time-keeping in the rhythm (nobody will get lost) and play everything, including the percussion, as musical phrases. And perhaps some of these things were discovered during the rehearsing on that very afternoon.

The occasion was also quite a contrast to the first rehearsal Ornette Coleman had held in New York over two years ago—a hurried, nervous affair (nearly panicky for a couple of the players) on the bandstand at the Five Spot, sandwiched between a trip to the police for cabaret cards and an opening night, complete with invited press, that very evening.

They were playing again. During Bobby Bradford's solo, a visitor touched his ear lobe and nodded toward the trumpeter, smiling, in indication of how well the young trumpeter was continuing to get with the melodic freedom of his music, and to playing with few guides but his own imagination. At the end of the piece, Coleman said to Moffett, "Yeah. But when you repeat the drum patterns you see they don't come around the same way every time."

"So when you're lost," Bradford cracked from across the room, "you're always lost at a different place!"

"Sure," smiled Ornette over the laughter. "So Bobby will keep track of where we are."

"See, Jimmy," Bradford continued to banter, "this is where he wants us to stop." He played a trumpet phrase. "In other words, take it phrase by phrase, but stop in the middle of the phrase." When the laughter had subsided again, "Seriously, Ornette, if we stop there we change the whole tune."

Coleman: "I guess that was a Sears-Roebuck stop. Let's find a Macy's stop." Turning to Moffett, "The rhythm you're playing now sounds like you're playing the piece. Play *against* the piece."

"I see. Counterpoint."

They ran through it again, and at the end Coleman turned again to Moffett, "That was good, but you ought to get another pattern to use in that piece too. And in that last little phrase you were still playing the melody. I don't even *want* it to sound like we're playing an arrangement."

Moffett: "Okay. On the turn-back, I'll play something different."

Coleman: "Aaaahhhhh!"

Moffett: "I know, I did it just half way in counterpoint that time. Let's try it again."

They began once more, still together, and still with no downbeat to be seen.

At the end, Coleman again turned to Moffett, "You hear that phrase you played at the end there? It implies another note. Your mind just fills it out even if you don't play that note. And don't think about the time at all, just about the accents."

Suddenly becoming very formal, and all but losing his Texas accent, Ornette Coleman turned to the room in general and said, "I wish it were possible to maintain the swing without making an obvious beat. I confess I don't know how to do it."

They were about to begin a new piece now when Coleman had announced by running off the first phrase, a sort of stop-and-go pattern. ("Wait till you hear this one!" whispered Mildred Fields.) "Will you please put some *names* to those things," pleaded Garrison, "so I can play them with you sometimes on my bass instead of waiting till you guys are halfway through the ensemble before I know what you're playing?"

Bradford laughed, "You know what he tells me? He turns his head and says, 'Let's play *la-de-do-doo-da* or *lee-doo-doe-doe-dum*,' and I say, 'Yeah!'"

Ornette: "Let's put numbers to them. C. M. can keep the numbers."

They all laughed. "That won't work! You will have to ask him for the number to *la-de-dah-do,* and it's the same thing all over again."

"There's *one* with a title we know," said Garrison, "Let's play the one you call *The Idiot.*" He hums.

Bradford: "Is *that* the name of that one?"

Coleman: "Yeah. I named it for the movie—of the Russian novel, you know. I thought the melody was the way the hero was."

Garrison: "Ornette, we ought to change the title to *Simple* or something like that. Suppose there are some idiots out here. They might not like it."

Coleman: "Suppose there are some on the bandstand!" laughing.

Bradford: "Well, *I* don't feel a draft!" (*1961*)

ॐ

MULLIGAN AND DESMOND
IN THE STUDIO

Studio A at RCA Victor Records is a large rectangular room, and recording engineers will tell you they get a very special sound there. If the group of musicians is a lot smaller than the room they install baffle boards and place their mikes carefully, and the sound they get is still special. The four-man group that Victor engineer Mickey Crofford was to record in Studio A on a warm summer evening was small in size, but not small in fame or talent—saxophonists Paul Desmond (who, of course, does most of his playing with Dave Brubeck) and Gerry Mulligan, plus bass and drums. And they were to improvise freely around arrangements written by Mulligan, which he had kept modest and flexible, with plenty of room for solo invention.

Like most jazz recording dates, this one combined constant pressure, banter, and even levity with utter seriousness, hard work, and musical accomplishment.

Desmond was early and by 7 p.m. he was seated in the engineer's booth just off Studio A. The booth is also a rectangular room, smaller than Studio A, with elaborate tape recorders and control boards at one end, and a comfortable visitors' area with chairs, couches, and a table at the other. From this booth there is a clear view of the rest of Studio A through the wide glass panel which runs along one end.

Desmond was going over some of Mulligan's scores with A & R man George Avakian, who was producing the date, and Avakian's associate, composer Bob Prince. As usual, the alto saxophonist was dressed in a neat brown Ivy League suit, white shirt, tie, and fashionably heavy-soled shoes. Also as usual, his suit was slightly in need of a press, his shirt a bit rumpled, and his shoes not recently shined.

Avakian seemed vaguely worried—for no good reason, but Avakian usually seems worried at the start of a recording date. Desmond seemed serious; Prince, confident. And Crofford was busy in the studio and in the booth with his microphones, switches, and dials.

Suddenly, all heads bobbed up as a knock on the glass and a broad grin revealed that Mulligan had arrived in Studio A. In contrast to Desmond, he was dressed in a pair of khaki slacks, a sports shirt, and a thick cardigan sweater. He was obviously ready to go to work: ready to exchange his black shoes for the white sneakers he was carrying, and to take his baritone sax out of its canvas sack and start playing.

Desmond had selected the Modern Jazz Quartet's Connie Kay as his drummer, and Kay entered almost on Mulligan's heels, waving his greetings and going immediately to work setting up his drums. Bassist John Beale, who had arrived soon after Desmond, was quietly running over his part to Kay's right. Kay had just returned from San Francisco with the Quartet. "Glad I finally got to you, Connie," said Desmond, crossing from the booth to the studio. "I was about to send up a skywriter—Connie Kay call Paul Desmond."

Crofford had placed music stands and high stools for the two horns facing the rhythm, with Desmond's alto on one stereo microphone and Mulligan's baritone on the other. Avakian—busy enough to be just now grabbing his supper, an oversized and somewhat over-drippy sandwich—was seated with pencils, note paper, and a stop watch beside Crofford's complex array of knobs, switches, and dials.

There had to be at least one run-through to test balance and mike placement. "We'll try one, okay?" said Avakian into his microphone, as Mulligan turned to Desmond with a mock serious frown to remark, "And please try not to play your best chorus now."

"Yeah, I'll save it," he answered, perhaps implying that he really had no control over the matter.

The piece was *Easy Living*, with Mulligan carrying the melody, Desmond inventing a countermelody behind him and taking the first solo. The performance was promisingly good, but Prince and Crofford decided there was too much mike on Kay's cymbal, and went into the studio to move things around a bit.

After another partial run-through, Avakian asked, "Want to tape one to see how it sounds?" But Paul and Gerry had their heads together over the music sheets.

"Try that last ensemble bridge again," Mulligan was saying. "You have the melody. It's the part down there at the bottom of the page." He pointed. "It could be a little more legato sounding." Desmond looked it over.

"I just wrote those notes in so you could see the pattern," Mulligan reminded Beale. "You don't have to play anything."

"Suppose I blow what you're playing along with you?" They tried it, and everyone commented that it sounded good.

"Want to tape one?" asked Desmond, affirming Avakian's suggestion. "We can figure out from the playback what's wrong."

In a few minutes there was a preliminary take of *Easy Living* on tape, and after the last note of the playback had echoed through the studio, it was obvious that this was going to be a relaxed and productive record date. Even Avakian seemed convinced of it. Mulligan had played with buoyancy, Desmond with fluent melodic ideas, and the impro-

vised counterpoint had had fine emotional and musical rapport. As one visitor said, "Yeah, tonight they're going to
play!"

As saxophonist of the Brubeck Quartet, Desmond is in a
rather odd position, for his talents are more respected by
musicians and critics than those of his pianist-leader. There
is, in fact, constant wonder in the trade as to why Paul
doesn't leave Dave and go off on his own. At the same time,
Desmond is of a cooler and more lyric persuasion than some
of the hard-blowing funk merchants who sell well on records nowadays, which puts him out of fashion in certain circles. Mulligan is something of an elder statesman as things
go in jazz: his popularity dates from the early fifties and the
days of the Mulligan Quartet. Since then he has held a large
following, while leading both large and small groups. Recently there has been as much talk of Mulligan the movie
actor (*The Subterraneans, Bells Are Ringing*) and of Mulligan the Broadway composer (a promised musical version
of *Happy Birthday* for Judy Holiday, who is to contribute
the lyrics) as about Mulligan the jazzman.

Several visitors and friends were in the booth by now.
And each time the door to Studio A was opened, the grind-
ing monotony of a rock and roll date being held next door
in Studio B assaulted the ears. It soon developed that some
rather illustrious jazzmen were involved in that music next
door, and their aesthetic escape proved to be frequent brief
visits over to the Desmond-Mulligan session to hear what
was going on.

After a good version of *Easy Living* had been put on tape,
there was some banter in the studio about, "Okay, that's it.
Everybody come back the same time tomorrow." And there
was some serious unwinding over Cokes, while Connie Kay
pulled out one of several hamburgers he had brought with

him. But discussion of the music didn't stop, and Mulligan was soon demonstrating a point, seated at the piano that stood in the far end of the studio.

Desmond said he wasn't sure he had quite done his best by *Easy Living,* and requested they try a slightly faster tempo—that they "make it a little brighter," as he put it— and all agreed to try the piece again. Just then Avakian threw his switch inside the booth and announced over the studio loudspeakers, "Gentlemen, I hate to say this, but I suggest you tune up a little."

"What? How could you even imply such a thing?" protested Mulligan with affected seriousness. And he carried his heavy horn over to the piano again to correct the matter.

When the tapes were rolling, Mulligan felt free enough to do some improvising even in his written parts.

At the end of the new take, before anyone had spoken, there was silent acknowledgment that it was the best yet. "Fine," said Avakian into his mike. "Want to hear it back?"

Mulligan again affected his cantankerous tone. "It's bad enough making these things without having to listen to them." He turned to Desmond, bobbing his eyebrows à la Groucho Marx, "Right? That a good attitude?" And a moment later, "Well, Paul, what other tunes do you know?"

"I know *Melancholy Baby.*"

"Who are you? Tex Beneke?" Desmond whispered quickly.

As Desmond improvised his solo, Mulligan again did his side-to-side strut. Then, with the tape still rolling and Desmond still soloing, Mulligan signaled to the rest of the group for a round of four-bar phrases from player to player, before he and Desmond went into the counterpoint choruses that finish the piece. An arrangement changed even while it was being recorded. They played the "fours," and as the saxophones were restating the theme at the end, Mulligan began to improvise and merely suggest the melody with a few key notes, as Desmond was playing it in full. It was an effective idea. This was really becoming a cooperative two-man date.

At the end of the take, Mulligan registered approval by turning his heavy horn horizontal and laying it across a raised knee. Paul entered the booth and asked almost shyly, "Where'd that coffee come from? Is it a local concern?"

Soon they were listening to a playback of a Mulligan blues they later decided to call *Blight of the Fumble Bee,* and a few minutes later they were running through the arranged parts of *All the Things You Are.* As they finished the conservative Bach-like ending Paul asked, "Isn't that a little daring?"

"Maybe," Mulligan countered. "It'll go okay in the Middle West."

As all this talk filtered through the open studio microphones into the visitors' booth someone muttered, "Maybe those two are trying to work up some kind of act. The bantering, and this Alphonse and Gaston about who's got the first solos and who has the melody and who the harmony. Maybe they could take it on tour."

"Connie," Desmond was saying, "do you remember the tempo of the last take you did?" Kay started to brush his snare drum with perfect memory, and unbelievable lightness.

On another *All the Things You Are* at a faster tempo, Paul seemed to be more comfortable. Gerry had been better at the slower one. Their only musical disagreement so far.

In a final take of *All the Things You Are,* Mulligan was smiling broadly as Desmond went into his opening "break" over suspended rhythm, and then invented a lyric solo as the beat resumed. He was still playing hunched over his horn, but this time he was allowing himself a slight motion of the legs in time to his improvising.

At the end, everyone seemed pleased with the performance. But the playback revealed a once-in-a-thousand accident: one of the microphones had briefly cut off during the counterpoint, and some bass notes didn't get on the tape. Desmond was especially disappointed, and for a moment looked as if he didn't want to play any more.

With their heads together, Avakian and Prince decided they could rerecord the bass part later and blend in the few missing notes, saving the performance.

"Otherwise, Bob," said Avakian, as everyone's relief settled in, "did you ever see a more relaxed and easy date?" Mulligan had again sat at the piano and was somehow running through a Mexican waltz, alternating it with some raucous low-down blues.

The ending Mulligan had designed for *Stardust* was rather complicated but Connie Kay had it after one explanation, and with no music sheet to refer to.

Mulligan said after a run-through: "Did you play a B flat there instead of a B natural?"

Desmond: "Um huh."

Mulligan: "Goodness gracious!"

As the take started, there was a fluent opening exposition by Mulligan, and it was evident from his first phrase that *Stardust* has a special meaning for him; he became so involved in his playing that at first he didn't hear Avakian calling out that there was not enough tape on the machines to finish the piece, that they had to put on another reel before making a full take.

On the next try, more new ideas rolled out of Mulligan's horn, and then Avakian waxed philosophical. "Very good! But it always seems to me if you get a very good one you should try another. A very good one may be a sign that an excellent one is on the way."

"Well, I don't hear anything *dramatic* about it," said Desmond quietly, "but otherwise it was very good."

They did *Stardust* again, and Mulligan's involvement was unabated. At one particularly delicate turn of phrase, a visitor in the booth yelled out. And in the studio Paul indicated his pleasure by smiling and pretending to conduct Kay and Beale, waggling his right forefinger in the student conductor's double-triangle 1-2-3-4, 1-2-3-4.

At the end, as they heard it played back, Mulligan smiled and laughed aloud at one of Desmond's phrases, and he danced a bit during the ensemble.

When the speakers were silent again, Desmond said quietly, "I think it's about time to amble on home, for me, anyway."

Mulligan started to play his theme song. And Kay had his cymbals almost packed away.   (*1963*)

VIDEOTAPING WITH DUKE

The final rundown and television taping of the show was scheduled for 1:00 p.m. No one was late. No one, that is, except the man who was supposed to bring Duke Ellington's suit, and he held things up considerably.

By 12:50 p.m. Ellington himself was moving down the hall toward WNEW-TV Studio 1. Inside, technicians were moving lights and cameras and chatting. And musicians were chatting, mostly, as usual, on the quantity and quality of last night's sleep. Tom Whaley, the Ellington orchestra's staff copyist of many years, was present, looking distinguished and carrying a home-movie camera, which he put to frequent use during the afternoon. Billy Strayhorn arrived, loaded down with a beige raincoat and the morning *Times*. Johnny Hodges was strolling around, occasionally twirling the instrument strap that hung at his neck.

The orchestra's chairs were set up, saxes on a raised platform to the left, brass similarly to the right, with Ellington's piano, Sam Woodyard's drums, and Major Holley's bass centered to the rear. The setup made a kind of inverted U, and it would allow the cameras to move in close to the sections and the individual players. Producer Robert Herridge and director Arnee Nocks had five cameras on the floor.

Trumpeter Cootie Williams arrived as several of the brass men were casually taking their places at music stands. But the milling around hadn't stopped yet. Nat Hentoff was talking with Harry Carney near the saxophones' platform. And Herridge was on the studio floor now, inconspicuous except for his clothes—a rough blue denim shirt, a pair of rumpled khaki trousers, and yellow work shoes.

As the early proprietor of *Camera 3,* an experimental television show done by the New York station of the Columbia Broadcasting System, WCBS-TV, Herridge had sought to discover what things would come across effectively on the small television screen and how they could be made more effective. He often presented jazz on *Camera 3.*

Subsequently, as producer of *The Lively Arts* for CBS, Herridge was responsible, with technical advisers Whitney Balliett and Hentoff, for the show called "The Sound of Jazz," a program that had featured Count Basie, Thelonious Monk, Red Allen, Billie Holiday, Pee Wee Russell, Jimmy Rushing, and Gerry Mulligan, among others. Herridge had become convinced that the best presentation of jazz was informal, with a minimum of comment and a close concentration by the cameras on the deep involvement of the musicians as they played—physical involvement that manifested psychological involvement as well.

Later, for CBS syndication to local outlets, the *Robert Herridge Theater* offered a program by Miles Davis with an orchestra led by Gil Evans, a program featuring Ben Webster and Ahmad Jamal, and a ballet on "Frankie and Johnny" for Melissa Hayden with music by Charlie Mingus and featuring Jimmy Rushing.

Currently, Herridge is taping a group of shows, some drama and some musical, for New York presentation—and then for national syndication—on WNEW-TV, the New York City television outlet of the Metromedia Corporation. One of these was to be an hour by Ellington, to be shown September 2 and 6. Again, Hentoff was serving as technical adviser, and one of his first acts was to persuade Herridge and director Nocks to have the Ellington orchestra's second-in-command, Strayhorn, in the engineering booth. Strayhorn would give specific musical cues, signals on what was happening and about to happen, throughout the taping, these to be relayed by headphones on the studio floor.

Things were beginning to settle down on the studio floor. One of the men was attaching a typed sheet of instructions to the side of his camera. A piano tuner was doing a final checking of the concert grand that Ellington was to use. Ellington was not on the floor now, but suddenly Harry Carney's baritone sound cut through the buzz of the room, and Cootie was warming up (using his plunger, by the way, even for this), playing *From Here to Eternity*.

Around these two sounds the Ellington orchestra gathered.

At 1:15 p.m., one of the trombonists told a joke that set the whole brass platform laughing. Over in a corner Hentoff explained to a friend that a few weeks before there had been some trouble in getting to Ellington—that is, to get through to him via agents and managers, and to get him to sit down and discuss a purely instrumental hour's presentation of his music for television. Ellington had also agreed, but with some apparent reservations, that the group could dress informally for the show. "All right," he said "the men can wear their own suits, but we'll bring the new uniforms along just in case."

The show was to begin with a full performance of *Take the "A" Train,* featuring Williams. Then four separate musical sections were to follow. And the idea this afternoon was to take things singly, to run through one section at a time and then tape it.

In the first portion would be the current Ellington medley of three of the best early Ellington–Bubber Miley pieces, *Black and Tan Fantasy, Creole Love Song,* and *The Mooche,* followed by a version of *The Opener,* with solos by Paul Gonsalves, Buster Cooper, and Cat Anderson. In the second section, there would be a version of the extended *Tone Parallel to Harlem.*

The third section would be taped last, since its length was the most flexible. It was to include a piece Ellington worked up with the orchestra at the previous day's rehearsal, which he punningly titled *Metro-media,* followed by *Jam with Sam,* both featuring extended soloing. Finally, they would go back to run down and tape the third section with two Hodges features, *Passion Flower* and *Things Ain't What They Used To Be,* followed by the Ellington feature *Kinda Dukish* leading into *Rockin' in Rhythm.*

"Danny, baby, up on the lights!" a man in a tweed hat shouted. Stagehands had drawn a pale blue curtain backdrop around three sides of the studio and suddenly everything looked orderly, bright, and vaguely unreal.

". . . just as soon as Duke finishes shaving. . . ." The words drifted up in reply from somewhere in the crowd.

"Fellas in the band"—it was Nocks, the director, now on the floor in the center of things—"we'd like you to be dressed the way you're going to be when we tape. We want to see about the lighting and so forth."

To his left someone was checking the sound on Ellington's voice microphone. "Yeah, I hear you now."

And then Ellington was back in the studio, temporarily in a tan jacket and a blue knit sports shirt and no tie. (So they were still waiting for his suit.) Herridge was leaning over the piano with Tom Whaley at his side. Whaley sat down to roll out an old sentimental ballad to everyone's amusement. Then Strayhorn sat on the piano bench and did the same ballad with some fine, archaic tremolos.

Then a characteristic descending run of notes announced that Ellington himself was now at the keyboard.

The lights went down, and the tension went up. A cameraman shouted, "Arty, baby . . ." and a light man heard, "Stand by with me, Danny. I'll cue you."

Ellington started to improvise on the first eight bars of "A" Train. Woodyard came in under him. The lights came up quickly as the main camera backed away, taking the whole band. Suddenly over the loudspeaker, a voice from the control room shouted, "Hold it, Duke! Hold it."

"I wasn't rehearsing," he answered calmly. "Is this mike on? You'd better test it."

There was a conference in the center of the floor on lights and camera movements. . . . "You kill the lights except on Duke. He plays. Then you bring them up fast when the band comes in. At the same time, the camera moves back fast to take in everybody."

In the background of all this, Ellington was striking a slow, broodingly impressionistic series of piano chords.

Then: "Okay, fellows. Stand by. Duke, stand by, please."

Everything went as it was supposed to. Ellington approached the finish of his introduction, the lights came up, and the camera backed away to take in the whole band. Williams stepped to the center for his solo. His sound had a burred edge even on open horn. He began in a kind of paraphrase tribute to Ray Nance's old *"A" Train* solo and then went off on his own. The saxes sounded fine. Williams played his darting coda.

Then the urbane Ellington faced his voice microphone and began to announce the medley of early pieces. He didn't get far—"Hold it, hold it. We lost a light. And if he steps up that way for his solo, he's in the way of the camera."

Another conference of technicians.

In the control room, one monitor screen showed a peaceful shot of Ellington, his head on his arms, resting across the top of the piano.

They began it again, and during the opening chorus of *"A" Train,* the superimposed title flipped by: A PORTRAIT IN MUSIC/DUKE ELLINGTON AND HIS ORCHESTRA.

"Beautiful opening!" somebody said. Nocks was crosscutting from one camera that was close up on Williams to another trained on the saxes, as the players exchanged phrases. Nocks spoke firmly to an assistant, who in turn spoke to the cameramen on the floor through their headsets: "Stand by Camera one! Take one! Stand by three. Take three!" Then he instructed the lighting director, who in turn spoke to his men on the floor through phones. And to the sound man, who instructed his men on the mikes and the booms on the floor. In the control room, it seemed a finely controlled roar of shouts and orders. But none of this technical turmoil reached the players, and the show was coming out orderly on the monitor screen.

Williams began the *Black and Tan-Creole Love Song-Mooche* medley. Then Rolf Ericson came in, also plunger-

style. Then Russell Procope on clarinet. All five cameras
were trained on him from different angles: his face, his embouchure, his fingers . . . medium shot, full length. Nocks
cued the various angles as his solo unfolded. Then there
were three clarinets on *The Mooche*—Procope, Carney, and
Jimmy Hamilton. ("Hal, are they all on the mike?") Then
Lawrence Brown, giving his own kind of lyric elegance to
the current role as the orchestra's plunger trombonist. Then
Williams ended it, with the clarinets holding a long, im-
passioned note under him.

"He's going back pretty far for those pieces," someone remarked quietly on the sidelines.

"Well, that's basic American music, man. What else could
be? Charles Ives?"

The Opener—and Gonsalves, Cooper, and Anderson
stepped to the center for swift solos.

So they had run through the opening and the first section.

Ellington stepped over to consult with Cooper about a
certain point in *The Opener*. Williams, somewhat aloof so
far this day, joined in with a point about a change of key.

"Any problems?" a late arrival asked Hentoff.

"No, these men are all pros," he said.

No one seemed to be in charge half the time, and no one
needed to be.

"Are we having an across-the-street break?" somebody
asked, as if to contradict Hentoff.

"Lock the doors!" he got in mock answer from across the
room.

Whaley was at the keyboard again, joined this time by
Hamilton and Hodges. Sound men and camera men were
discussing what they had seen so far and hoped to capture
soon during the actual taping. Ellington and Herridge were
in a conference in a corner. Woodyard approached a table

that held an endless and constantly renewed supply of coffee and pastries. He looked rather sad when he couldn't find a plain glass of cold water.

Ellington's suit still had not arrived. Well, why not run down the second section now, and then tape both in succession later?

"Let's go! On the stand, fellows!"

Soon Ellington was speaking into the rehearsal camera with a sly half-smile: "And now Harlem, or rather our *Tone Parallel to Harlem*. . . . Harlem is very close to us. . . . A lot of nice people live there. Oh, some naughty people too. But Harlem is such a nice place it even has a minister for congressman. . . . We hear it late one Saturday night and early Sunday morning. We start this by having Cootie Williams pronounce the word 'Harlem' on his trumpet."

Williams picked it up and then began to pass the phrase to the whole brass section. Ellington was at the center of the orchestra, conducting with both arms. Then Gonsalves was soloing, and Ellington held a mike toward his horn. Woodyard, alert to the tricky tempo changes, whipped up the "Latin" section. Then Lawrence Brown, with a felt mute on his horn, stated the Sunday morning theme. Then Procope, Hamilton, and Carney, all on clarinets, wove a variation on it.

"I'm sorry, I'm sorry. Hold it, Duke. Cut!"

There was a pause, as Ellington asked, "What letter is that?" The technicians settled their problems in a moment.

"Duke, can we go back to Lawrence Brown's trombone solo?" Yes. (They learned this score too in the previous day's rehearsal, it seems.)

"Yeah, what letter is that?" Ellington asked again.

Brown stood up again and restated his theme. Again the clarinets recomposed it. As they played, Ellington stood at the center, apparently examining a fingernail. Then he was waving and gesturing the group into the finale. Left arm, right arm, left arm, right. Both arms.

"Take five!"

It wasn't exactly a break for everyone, although several players headed for the hall and the bank of telephones against a back wall. There were various conferences about camera angles, lighting positions, and the rest. To the rear of the studio, Whaley took some kidding about his movie camera: "In case their tape doesn't come out, you can always sell them what you're getting, I suppose?"

"You know I took some wonderful stuff on the set when we were working on *Paris Blues*," Whaley said. "And the developer sent back some movies of a kid's birthday party. I wrote and wrote but never did get my film back."

Around the room one could hear: "They're going to take longer than they planned at this."

"When do you think they'll wrap it up?"

"Do you know it's Duke's birthday today?"

"Hey, Duke's clothes came! Now we'll move!"

Soon, Ellington entered in a blue suit, light television blue shirt, dark blue tie, and blue suede shoes.

"Stand by, fellows! From the top of the show!"

Nocks was on the floor for a final word with the cameramen.

"Let's make this one———"

"Hold your shot. Is Duke ready?"

"Hal, let us know when———"

"Get ready—wait one second."

"Okay, Arnee? Okay, roll the tape."

Ellington's introduction approaches its end. The camera quickly pulls back.

No lights.

"Dammit!"

"Okay, again. Fade 'em down. Cue, Duke."

The taping brought the music fully to life; no one was coasting now. On the medley, the cameras caught Lawrence Brown in fine detail. One had the movement of his face muscles. Another, his hands, manipulating plunger and slide. Another, the slight but telling movements of his body in time with his phrases.

On *The Opener,* Gonsalves crouched. Cooper's embouchure worked rapidly. And Cat Anderson was caught by one camera in laughing amusement at his own high note ending, the moment after he finished his solo.

"Beautiful ending!" someone shouted.

"There was only one little thing I didn't like in the whole segment." It was Herridge's voice; he didn't go on to say what.

Inside the studio, the assemblage was still subdued and quiet until someone shouted, "Take five!"

It seemed considerably less than five minutes later when the shout went up in the hall outside the studio door, "Okay, everybody! We're gonna tape *Harlem* now!"

The musicians reentered the studio and moved toward the stands.

Ellington sat in a spotlight at the center of the group, awaiting his cue that the tape was running. He joked mildly with the band under his breath. Then on his cue, he did his speech about Harlem.

Two cameras catch Cootie's opening pronouncement: *"Har-lem. Har-lem. . . ."*

One was suddenly aware of the careful attention to sound the crew was giving this show, a quite unusual thing for television, even on a musical program. There were seven mikes for the music alone.

Ellington conducted with no score of course, encouraging, quieting, cuing. Woodyard's hard tom-tom produced a strong "Yeah!" from the leader.

Then, as the lyric Sunday morning theme was unfolded, first by Brown and then by the clarinets, one camera caught Ellington, suddenly in repose, with his head resting on his arms across the piano. The Duke won't be in church this morning; he overslept.

At the end, a simple "Okay, Duke," quietly spoken through the loudspeaker, hardly gave an indication of how pleased men in the control room were with the sequence.

"Every shot came off right," Hentoff remarked, smiling, on entering the studio.

At 4:35 p.m. the piano tuner had finished rechecking the instrument, and there was a cry of "Okay, fellows, let's run through the final section now."

Into the cold camera, Ellington explained that *Passion Flower* featured Johnny Hodges, and that Robert Herridge felt that the meaning of a "passion flower" was better experienced than explained. Then he gestured to his right and turned. And saw no Hodges.

"Where are you going to be?"

"Well, I'm over here."

"Oh."

As Hodges segued from *Passion Flower* into *Things Ain't What They Used To Be,* Whaley sat in one corner copying out some parts for the new piece, *Metro-media.*

When they finished *Rockin' in Rhythm,* an inside joke sent up a roar from the orchestra. As it died down, Nocks announced loudly, "Please be in your seats in exactly one hour. Then we will tape this section, time what we have, and then do the third section."

About ten minutes later, most of the musicians had left to eat supper. But Cat Anderson was still around, watching the tape playback on a monitor in the studio. He laughed again at his own ending to *The Opener* and at the shot of himself looking surprised.

"This is even better than the show we did in England," he said. "Of course, they only used three cameras."

"Hey, there's a camera showing behind Cootie in that shot!"

"Herridge doesn't care. He wants it informal, and he doesn't see any sense in pretending to the viewer that there aren't cameras around. So if one camera picks up another, what about it?"

Ellington watched the playbacks on another monitor, seated in a chair in the director's booth. His face was sober and did not give away his feelings much. Behind him, a semicircle of cameramen and light men were more vocal.

"Hey, look at that shot George got!"

"Eddie, did you see that!"

"That's good, that's good. . . ."

"Sure I got the cue right. I'm old enough to know that piece for a long time."

By 6:15 p.m. everyone was back, feeling cheery and well fed. *Rockin' in Rhythm* did rock, and they finished the whole show by eight.

Then there was a birthday party.

"How old am I—fifty-five?" Ellington asked, smiling, and lopping off ten years.

It was a surprise party; yet it probably surprised no one. Still, it was not the sort of thing one usually sees in a television studio.

But then, an hour of music by a great jazz orchestra, carefully produced, well photographed, and well recorded, is not the sort of thing one sees in a television studio, either. (*1964*)

MONK AT REHEARSAL

"What time does a ten o'clock rehearsal start?"

"Well, I think Jerome Richardson will be here soon. And Steve Lacy. They picked up their parts yesterday to take them home."

The speaker is Hall Overton. He is dressed in a rather baggy white shirt and dark trousers, standing next to a two-burner gas stove in the kitchen area of his midtown New York loft studio, three steep flights above its Sixth Avenue entrance, and as he finishes speaking he offers his visitor some coffee.

Out in the rather rugged two-room studio, two photographers are busy setting up their lights, attaching them to pipes and to the sides of the several bookcases that line one wall or placing them on the tops of the two upright pianos. Overton has a floor-through, which means the front windows would overlook Sixth Avenue if they were not largely covered by blinds against the morning sun. The two rooms are one in effect, since they are separated only by a wide arch. In the center of the rear room there are set up two rows of four chairs, plus as many music racks and stands as are available.

At 10:15 a.m. the first two players arrive. Thad Jones and Phil Woods are neatly dressed, and both look bright and wide awake. After greetings, Jones and Woods take chairs, get out their horns, look over their music, meanwhile exchanging stories about somebody's embouchure and somebody else's pet dog and cat.

Overton continues to prepare and offer coffee in the kitchen alcove. He explains, "We are going to do *Thelonious* and *Monk's Mood,* which are not too hard. We will be doing *Four in One* at the concert, but we can't rehearse it today because I don't have the score yet. And we have another tough one, *Little Rootie Tootie,* though it's not quite as hard as *Four in One.*"

"Didn't you do that at a Town Hall concert a few years ago?" Jones asks.

"Yeah. Monk misplaced the score, and I had to do it all over again. Of course, our instrumentation this time is different."

As Overton speaks, trombonist Eddie Bert arrives, quietly, as is usual with him.

The reason for the Thursday morning rehearsal is revealed in a poster on the side wall of the studio: "THE-LONIOUS MONK Orchestra at Carnegie Hall. Saturday, June 6 at 8:30 P.M." It is to be Monk's second concert of the season, a kind of follow-up to his much-praised evening at Lincoln Center the previous December.

Again, Overton had done the scores for the orchestra, working not only with Monk's themes but also with written variations based on Monk's recorded piano solos on a couple of the pieces—these are what make up the difficult portions of *Four in One* and *Little Rootie Tootie.*

It is the third such collaboration of Overton and Monk, the first being the 1959 Town Hall concert that Jones remembered.

As planned, the Carnegie concert is to open with a Monk solo. Then Monk's quartet is to play several pieces—the quartet currently consisting of Monk, tenor saxophonist Charlie Rouse, bassist Spanky DeBrest, and drummer Ben Riley. The orchestra is to appear in the second half, and the evening will end with a second Monk piano solo.

It is now about 10:25, and Steve Lacy has arrived.

"Of course, a ten o'clock rehearsal starts at eleven," somebody says.

Woods is playing the piano. Overton is explaining how jealously Monk guards his own scores: he usually asks for them immediately after a concert performance and puts them away at home but often can't find them again when he needs them.

At 10:30 Richardson enters, offering hearty and boisterous greetings to the others.

Overton is now going over a part with Bert. Nick Travis arrives, looking mildly genial as usual, and is soon in joking conversation with Jones. From time to time the phone rings, and Overton speaks quietly into the receiver, "Well, right now we're about to. . . ."

Rouse has still not arrived, but at about 10:35 the six horn men assemble in their chairs by unspoken agreement to begin the rehearsal. It turns out that the saxophones need a little more light on their parts, and some lamps get moved around.

"Hall, have you got a piece of sandpaper? This reed is a little . . ." It is Richardson. Lacy has a piece and passes it over.

Overton faces the group and indicates that they may as well start with the hard one, *Little Rootie Tootie.*

"Let's try it at this tempo right here," he says crouching slightly and patting his right foot. "I'll give you a measure and a half."

They begin the train whistle effect that opens the piece.

"Hold it! Steve, come down. Phil, I'd like you to accent the G flat and the A."

They start again. Halfway through the chorus Overton stops them again, saying:

"Phil, right there—you got the right sound. But hold it a bit and give it a little vibrato."

"Put a little crescendo on it?"

"Yeah, maybe like a dotted quarter."

The phone rings. "Hello. . . . He's not here. . . . I'm not sure—he should be here any minute."

They begin again: "One, two, three, four. Cut off at three. But get the swell."

"At the fifth measure of B," Overton says indicating a section of the score, "baritone, two trumpets, and trombone. Got it? Okay."

The four horns execute a fat chord.

"Now, all of it again. We are missing the tenor, an important sound here, of course."

They are also still missing a rhythm section, but an ensemble swing is definitely developing.

"That was right, but let's try it at B once more—in the sixth measure. That G should be louder. Now once more at B."

They have the opening chorus down now, and it is time to move to the hard part, the closing ensemble choruses based on Monk's solo. Overton indicates the section, saying, "Okay, let's get started at E."

Spontaneously, Jones and Travis begin the chorus with no cue from Overton, using the previous tempo. The others join. The phrases link together. There is laughter at one passage, caused by its difficulty—and its unexpected musical logic. Hall shouts "diminuendo" over the ending.

The group has awakened to a musical challenge. "Can we go back to I or J?" Richardson asks.

"Right now let's get this part here—you have to accent every one of those triplets," Overton says to the group generally.

A few minutes later Thad Jones is asking, "Let's start back at E again."

Overton agrees now. But before the group begins, Jones and Travis are running off one of the most difficult passages together.

"That was crazy!"

"It is kind of ignorant, ain't it?" says Jones, laughing broadly.

As they go through it again, Overton goes to the piano and stands at the keyboard, reaching down to add the continuing train whistle responses to the ensemble.

"Hey," Richardson says at the end, "it's moving! It'll walk by itself now!"

Rouse enters, to general greetings and a "Hey, Roustabout!" from Jones.

He takes his place between Richardson and Woods, and Overton asks if Woods can lend his instrument case for a substitute music stand.

Once more Jones and Travis begin the closing variations, and the group joins them. They have set the tempo faster this time. A mistake breaks up a couple of the players, but the music continues.

"Is that where you're going to put it?" asks Richardson about the new tempo.

"No," Jones replies. "Just to try it."

"Nothing wrong with it," Richardson responds. "Feels good up there too."

"Hey, let's tune up," says Overton going to one of the pianos to sound an A. After the general din, he takes his place in front of the group again, saying, "From the top, now that we've got everyone here."

Afterwards: "Once more, from the top. But didn't we get a train whistle sound on this introduction before?" He is addressing Woods, who had played *Little Rootie Tootie* at the Town Hall concert. His answer comes from all sides, as various of the players try wailing and bending their opening notes. Then there is one more run-through, and it comes off well.

"How about this way, Hall?" Jones asks, and then runs

off a slightly revised and reaccented version of one of the trumpet phrases. He has made the passage less pianistic, pronouncing it the way a brass man would.

"Fine—now at the end of your part," Overton continues to the group methodically, "I have written out four chords. We can use these for backgrounds. You play each three times, like the opening. Let's try the first one." He gives a downbeat. "Now the second." Another downbeat, followed by another triple wail.

"Man!" somebody interjects, "that's a weird sound."

At the end of the fourth, the sudden clanging and wailing sound of a fire engine swells up from the street below.

"That's the whistling sound we want!" says Richardson over general laughter.

They are about to set aside *Rootie Tootie* for the time being.

"Hall, can we have some coffee or something?"

"Sure." There is a break while coffee is prepared.

"Got anything to eat? I didn't get any breakfast."

"I think there's some cookies."

"That'll do fine."

"This music is hard to phrase right," Overton muses in the kitchen alcove.

"Yeah. So many of Monk's things are traditional, but he uses them in such an original way. If you play them the old way, they don't sound right at all."

At about 11:30 drummer Riley arrives with his set, apologizing for his lateness. He moves a little stiffly and explains that he caught a cold early in the week and then aggravated it by going out in the rain to pick up his daughter after school.

A couple of minutes later, Jules Colomby, who is producing the concert, enters. With him are Spanky DeBrest and Thelonious Monk. Monk walks in, staring rather vaguely in front of him and not looking at anyone in particular. He returns Thad Jones's greeting and twirls around in a kind of dance movement. Lacy approaches him, and they exchange greetings. Then for a moment he looks out of the back windows of the studio. Soon he speaks to Overton: "How's it going?"

"So far pretty good. There are some problems with the horns. . . ."

Monk is still in his hat and raincoat, which is buttoned all the way up tightly around his neck, the collar turned up.

DeBrest warms up by reading his part. Riley sets up his drums.

"Thelonious," Overton is saying, "I scored out some chords at the end of *Rootie Tootie*. When you hear them you might want to pick a couple for backgrounds for the solos."

Monk nods.

The coffee break is about over, and the group is reassembling in the chairs as Overton tries to set future rehearsals: "Let's have another tomorrow morning."

"I can't come," someone says. "I have to teach, and I have a job tonight that will keep me out late besides."

"Neither can I—I have a show to do," Bert says almost shyly.

"Maybe we could get substitutes for you two—wait a minute!" Overton remembers. "I can't either. I forgot I have something I can't break. Well, it'll just have to be Saturday morning before the concert. Here. Ten o'clock?"

There is general nodding.

"Then we'll have to get to the hall early to set a balance. We can get Carnegie during the afternoon for rehearsing, too, if we want."

"No, let's not rehearse in the afternoon. Our chops will be worn out before the concert."

"We ought to do *Thelonious* and *Monk's Mood* today," Overton says. "Shall we do them and then go back to *Little Rootie Tootie?*"

Monk is walking, pacing the room, skirting the musicians, dancing a little, waiting to hear. He still has his coat on, and his collar is still up.

They run down *Thelonious,* Monk's intriguing theme built around one note. At the end, Overton turns to Monk and says, "That goes faster than that, doesn't it?"

Monk moves to the piano, apparently to give the question a complete answer, and begins to play the piece himself, a bit faster, very forcefully, and with fascinating harmonies and successions of sounds pivoting off that one note.

At the end, Overton asks, "Are you going to take all the blowing on this?"

"Anybody can blow it if they know the chords."

"Well, did it sound okay?"

"Was everybody in tune?" Monk asks. "Yeah, it sounds okay."

Overton turns to the group again and says, "Let's decide about the solos later. Now we'll try *Monk's Mood.*"

As the players get out their parts, Overton confers with Monk.

"We'll do it this way," he says finally. "We'll begin with a solo chorus by Monk. Then the band. Then Charlie Rouse. Then Monk. Then the band again, and out."

As they go through *Monk's Mood* again, the composer moves to the rear of the group to listen and probably to have more room for his rhythmic pacing as well.

"Try for a feeling of triplets right here," Overton instructs. "Okay, from the top again."

Some of the players move their feet in a kind of suggested

6/8 time to get the proper feeling during the triplet passage.

"Is something wrong with your part there in the first eight?" Overton asks. "Let's see your copy, Charlie."

One more run-through, with Bert's trombone again opening up the theme and the group picking it up. They now have rehearsed their ballad for the evening, *Monk's Mood*.

"Okay, let's go on to *Rootie Tootie* again," Overton says. "Monk, I'd like you to hear those chords now. Maybe you could think about how you would like to use them for background?"

Monk nods. And paces. And turns. His tread is becoming heavier and more varied.

"Okay, here we go, chord number one."

A piercing collection of sounds.

"Now number two. Three times again. Number three. Number four."

Overton looks up at Monk, who continues stepping and turning.

"I think number one and number four work out," Overton says finally. "Maybe we can use them in the background. Okay, now from the top of *Rootie Tootie*."

They run through it once, and it goes well. As they are about to begin again, Overton says, "Hey, Thelonious . . . ," gesturing toward the piano.

Monk seems uninterested. He still has on his coat and hat and is perspiring, especially around the collar. Jones and Richardson start off again, with no signal from Overton, who crosses to the piano to play the continuing train whistle responses to the orchestra's figures. He is backed by accents from Riley.

At the end, Monk says, "Everybody ought to hold that last note."

"But fade it out gradually, right?" Overton asks.

"Yeah."

"Now for backgrounds to the solos. The last time we did it this way. For the first eight, we play A once. For the second eight nothing. Then play the bridge. Then lay out for the last eight. Then do it the other way."

"In other words," Woods says, "alternate eights."

"Yes, but first one way, then the other. See what I mean? Let's try it. Thad, you blow two choruses."

Jones starts to blow with the group for eight bars, then off on his own for eight, back with the group for eight more, and so forth. Jones is just riding along for rehearsal's sake, of course, but he sounds good.

"Don't use the last eight," comments Travis at the end, "because it's up an octave. Use the first there."

Monk's movements, feet complemented by flying elbows, are developing into a kind of tap dance. At the same time, he still seems to be executing counterrhythms and special accents to the piece as they play it. Overton crosses over to him for a quiet discussion—a discussion on cigarettes, one might think from the concentration with which both of them are smoking.

Moving back to the front of the group again, the orchestrator says, "We've got exactly a half hour left. We don't have the parts on *Four in One*. How would you like to spend it?"

"Let's work on *Tootie*," Jones says. "At E."

There is general agreement. But the musicians spend a short moment to chat and joke a bit beforehand; it is as if the group were gathering strength for a difficult task.

Then after a couple of minutes, Overton says, "Okay, here we go at E. One . . . two . . . one, two, three, four."

The choruses go well, but there are still rough spots.

"I want to take it at H."

To the rear, Monk is decidedly tap dancing now, in an unorthodox but effective way. The collar of his raincoat is quite wet. His face is still expressionless—or perhaps a bit solemn. And he seldom looks directly at anyone unless he is speaking to them—as if he were too shy to but not quite admitting it. He is listening, and his movements still seem to be a way of participating in the rehearsal—encouraging, feeling if it's right. From time to time, one or two of the players will turn to watch him briefly after a particularly heavy stomp or tap or a triplet.

"Could I have J, slower?" Overton asks, moving beside Riley, humming the band part and gesturing with his right hand to indicate snare accents.

"That's not the problem, playing that part there," suggests Richardson. "It's getting that accent right at a faster tempo."

"Once more this way, and then we'll do it fast."

As they go through it again, Overton lays his conductor's score aside and crosses to the piano. He sits down this time to play, and as he bends over the keys in playing Monk's part he almost takes Monk's piano position.

At the end, he turns to Woods and asks, "What do you think, Phil?"

"It's coming. Can we do the whole thing?"

"Good. Let's do it all, and, Thad, do two choruses solo, with the background. Then into E. Okay, right from the top. And Phil, you cut it off at the end, because you'll have to at the concert. They can all see you."

They play *Rootie Tootie* from the top, and suddenly the piece seems whole—from the opening ensembles, through the backgrounds through Jones's chorus, blowing into the variations at the end. The only thing missing is Monk.

"Hey, Phil," someone chides. "That wasn't a very classy cut-off."

"Don't listen to him—that was fine, Phil."

"Thanks a *lot!*"

"Okay," says Overton, smiling lightly at the banter. See you on Saturday at ten o'clock, here."

To the rear, Monk's percussive steps and patterns continue. (*1966*)

ᘒᕗ

THAD AND MEL AT THE VILLAGE VANGUARD

Seventh Avenue South in New York City is Seventh Avenue below 14th Street, a truck-and-taxi-laden street that courses through Greenwich Village. On the west side of Seventh, just below a street marked Murly Square, there is a canvas canopy leading from the sidewalk's edge to a neat, white double door. Above the canopy is a modest neon sign that announces "Village Vanguard."

Through the white doors, a steep stairway descends to the cellar, and at the foot of the stairs, a second door opens to a small, triangular, dimly lit basement room. This is the Vanguard, one of the best-known and longest-surviving night clubs in New York.

Inside, a slight, studious-looking young man is collecting $3 from each arriving customer. It is Monday, and Monday nights are special at the Vanguard. For the $3 admission, plus whatever else one may want to pay for drinks and food, one gets to hear the Thad Jones-Mel Lewis Orchestra live, and its most ardent admirers will tell you that the Thad Jones-Mel Lewis Orchestra is the best large jazz ensemble there is.

To the right and the left, the club's deep-red walls, decorated with scattered photographs and some ancient tubular instruments, lead one's eyes toward the point of the triangle, where sits the club's bandstand. Ordinarily, a quartet can look pretty crowded up there at the end of the Vanguard, but tonight somehow, there are fourteen chairs and music stands up there plus drums and piano.

It is 9:30 p.m. There are approximately six couples seated at the club's tiny circular tables in the center floor, or at the small rectangular ones against the walls. It's early as things go on a Vanguard Monday; the insiders know there is no real point in arriving until about ten.

Over the PA system, a recorded pianist is playing a Charlie Parker blues; the volume is turned low. A young girl seated against the east wall is saying to her date, loudly for some reason, ". . . off base *again!*" and topping it with an energetic giggle. The lights are dim, but clearly she is a redhead. By the entrance a waiter is explaining a complex chess move to the young doorman.

Pepper Adams, resembling a cheerful, businesslike owl, arrives, crosses to the bandstand, puts a manila folder on one of the front-row music stands, and disappears to the rear.

The "rear" of the Vanguard is at the lower east point of its triangle, an enclosed area behind the bar that somehow manages to contain the kitchen, the men's room, and a "backstage" area with a small table and a couple of chairs for the musicians for use between sets.

To the rear, a trumpet (or is it Thad Jones's cornet or a fluegelhorn?) warms up, clashing with the pianist on the loudspeakers. Another trumpet joins him—isn't that Richard Williams? The bartender briefly adds to the cacophony with a shaker full of mixed booze and ice.

Adams, laden with his baritone, heads for the bandstand. He is followed by Billy Mitchell with tenor saxophone and clarinet. The buzz of conversation is louder now, louder and expectant. A couple in their late fifties, in the company of a younger man and woman, arrive. The group is neatly and conservatively dressed, like most of the other customers.

As they are seated, a lean young man carrying a bass crosses the bandstand and introduces himself to trombonist Wayne Andre, who is opening his instrument case. The bassist is Miroslav Vitous, a young Czech of high reputation, substituting tonight for Richard Davis. As they leave the stand, Mel Lewis arrives, earnest and hurried, and rushes to the stage, where he removes a raincoat and starts setting up his drums. Thad Jones, now on the bandstand checking things out, stops to talk over an administrative point with his co-leader.

In a few minutes the musicians begin to head for the front of the clubroom. One or two drop by the bar or at tables to greet friends and regulars.

"Gimme a drink before the fight starts," someone says. The room is about two-thirds full now, and many of the customers are eyeing the entering musicians, intently or self-consciously. To the rear, one of the waiters, a white-haired man with a middle European accent is confiding to someone at the bar, "I opened this place, you know. Yeah, been here steady since the first night."

The first night for the Village Vanguard was in 1934. The club was started by Max Gordon, who still owns it and runs it and still comes in almost every night. Gordon, a short and usually pleasant man, whose round, sometimes cherubic and sometimes intent face is decorated above the ears by what remains of his curly white hair, will explain that he came to New York from Portland, Ore., and got his first job washing dishes in a cafeteria. When the Vanguard opened, it was at first a place where one might have heard Maxwell Bodenheim or Harry Kemp read their poetry, while young painters argued about politics or Georges Braque. A couple of years later, the entertainment was provided by a then-unknown group called The Reviewers: Judy Holiday, Adolph Green, and Betty Comden, with a young pianist named Leonard Bernstein.

Subsequently, the Village Vanguard offered folk music, from Leadbelly's southern U.S. songs to the Duke of Iron's Caribbean calypso; or it had cabaret songs with Eartha Kitt or Harry Belafonte; and comedy by Pearl Bailey and Wally Cox. And there were the Weavers, Robert Clary, Orson Bean—the list is long, and the subsequent successes are many. The club was a tourist attraction that was still considered a hip and "inside" place by New Yorkers themselves.

Fairly consistently, jazz was a part of the bill. Willie "The Lion" Smith worked with the calypso men. Drummer Zutty Singleton brought in a group. Jimmy Hamilton was featured. My own earliest memory of the club is seeing Roy Eldridge there for the first time in 1942 (and wondering when somebody was going to realize I was under age and throw me out).

About ten years ago, Gordon reversed his policy, putting jazz at the top of the bill and letting the folknicks (like the Brothers Four or the Clancy Brothers) and the comics (Mort Sahl, Mike Nichols and Elaine May, Lennie Bruce, Woody Allen, Irwin Cory) fill it out. Thus the Vanguard booked Miles Davis, Horace Silver, Thelonious Monk, Gerry Mulligan, the Modern Jazz Quartet, Jimmy Giuffre, Anita O'Day, Charlie Mingus, Bill Evans (a regular), Stan Getz, Carmen McRae.

The Monday night sessions with the Jones-Lewis band began about a year and a half ago. Gordon and disc jockey-entrepreneur Alan Grant heard that such a band was out there somewhere rehearsing and went to hear it. The band has been playing, usually to packed houses, on the club's off night ever since, and even for a few weeks as the regular attraction.

Jones sits doodling now at the piano. "Snookie Young!" someone greets the lead trumpeter to the rear of the stand. Jerome Richardson, a forceful man in any context, enters with a rack of horns and heads for his seat. Tom McIntosh sits at the end of the line of four trombones. In the house, some musician visitors are beginning to arrive, as they usually do on these Mondays. Joe Henderson is leaning against a back wall. Guitarist Atilla Zoller sits near the end of the bar, smiling as usual.

On the bandstand, the numbers of the sequence of tunes for the first set are being voiced around. "I think the competition got us this evening," says Richardson, nodding at the few empty tables to the rear of the room.

Suddenly there is the din of a wild tune-up, as Jones stands in front of the ensemble clapping both for order and to give a tempo.

"It's two hundred twelve and *then* sixteen!" someone is loudly explaining to his neighbor through the sound. Then out of the chaos, all is order as the first piece begins. All eight brass are playing forte, and the small room is full of sound, yet somehow it is not loud, only exhilarating. Thad solos, telling his story with an easy fluency. The band comes back in. Figures well up, spread across the ensemble and then subside. The group shouts, and whispers with the same conviction, and the music seems constantly to move forward with a kind of graceful relentlessness.

"Well, all right!" comments Richardson while the last note is still subsiding. Jones thanks the audience for its applause and the microphone fades and crackles on him a bit as he announces that the piece had been *Low Down*. Next, he says, will be a ballad, *All My Yesterdays*, to feature trom-

bonist Garnett Brown. Brown grins, shakes his head, and
points energetically to Andre on his left.

A young man says to his date at a back table, "That's
him! See him?" He is indicating one of the saxophonists.
"He's here this time. But no matter who shows up, the band
still sounds great."

During the ballad, a couple comes through the entrance.
He looks to be about thirty; she looks to be sixty; both look
like middle-class suburbanites. The crowd, its attention as
usual centered on the band, shows a scattered annoyance
as a waiter shows them to a table and asks if they want to
order anything.

Five minutes later, the band is into a medium-tempo
piece. Jones is rocking from one foot to another, clapping
softly—he is conducting, dancing, encouraging, and enjoy-
ing himself, all at once. Then tenor saxophonist Lou Taba-
kin is into an energetic Coltrane-esque solo, which has the
enthusiastic attention of the audience and the bandsmen. A
bit later, behind Jones's solo, all twelve horns are executing
a figure that kicks along but doesn't blast.

The cornetist-leader announces that the final selection
will be a blues. Richardson begins it entirely alone, with
several fast choruses. On Jones's signal, Vitous's bass joins
him and then Lewis's drums. Each entrance paradoxically
relieves the tension and then sets up a tension of its own.
The ensemble enters. Then, suddenly, trombonists Brown
and Andre are trading phrases. Then Brown solos. Andre
rejoins him. Brown drops out again. The relay effect is stun-
ning.

Richardson returns, and the trombones back him with a
tonally oblique figure that sets trumpeter Young to grin-
ning broadly. The dynamics duck way down for Chick
Corea's piano solo, but the crowd still listens.

Then Brown is up for still another solo. He manages to

bean Richardson with his slide. It gets a laugh, of course, from the band and the patrons alike.

The piece ends with some fine trumpet shakes on top, and the applause is enthusiastic and sustained. Clearly this band has its following, probably the most attentive following to be found in any club today.

The musicians leave the stand, but even now they look quite ready for another set. Jones joins some friends at a table. Adams and Lewis chat with a couple of fans. Over by the bar, Zoller is explaining a fine point of amplification to Max Gordon. Through the door comes trombonist Eddie Bert, horn in hand, ready to play the next set with the group.

A middle-aged fan, seated at the end of the bar nursing a beer, is holding forth, "Now the Fatha Hines band of the mid-forties—that had Bird and Dizzy, you know. Bird was playing tenor. That was quite a band. Then there was the Eckstine band. He had *everybody*—Dizzy, Fats Navarro, Kenny Dorham, even Miles, who was pretty young then, and Bird, Dexter Gordon, Lucky Thompson, Art Blakey. That was quite a band. Then there was Dizzy's band. . . ." He trails off momentarily, but then turns to the bartender abruptly, saying, "But *this* band! . . ."   (*1967*)

RECORDING MILES DAVIS

The administrative offices of Columbia Records are now located in the parent company's externally handsome CBS Building on New York's Avenue of the Americas. But for the purposes of recording, the old, reliable Columbia studios still seem to serve best. Thus, on a morning last winter, a Miles Davis recording session was set for the venerable Studio B, on East 52nd Street near Madison.

The date was called for 10:00, but by 9:40, Davis was there, his thin, broad-shouldered frame comfortably dressed in a long-sleeved, knit sport shirt and a pair of corduroy trousers. He was lounging casually on a chair in the control room, but he was obviously anxious to get to work. The day before he had not been so optimistic. "We may just end up rehearsing, or sitting around looking at each other," he had commented with a not unusual edge of humor in his voice.

Davis is notoriously taciturn on the bandstand, disinclined to announce his numbers or to acknowledge applause. But the more private Miles Davis is a talkative man whose conversation is a stream of anecdotes, free-associated reminiscences, and outspoken reactions and opinions, most of which are delivered with a kind of shared, ironic wit that tempers an occasional bitterness.

Columbia's engineer Frank Laico, with two assistants, was threading tapes, adjusting dials, and checking the placement of the battery of microphones on view through a glass panel in the large rectangular studio directly ahead. Davis meanwhile was commenting to guitarist George Benson: "When whites play with Negroes and can't play the music, it's a form of Jim Crow to me. Studio musicians—they're supposed to be able to play all kinds of music. So they should know what's going on in our music, too. One, two, three, four—anybody can do that. And if you don't do it, they don't believe the beat is still there." Davis was still smarting from the experiences of a previous session when an otherwise capable studio guitarist had failed him miserably. "I was so mad, they gave me a royalty check and I didn't even look at it."

This date, therefore, with Benson on guitar, was a kind of make-up for the previous session. Columbia is willing to devote much time and money to Davis's recorded output, and Miles Davis, for all the casual air with which he goes about it, is a careful craftsman. He has been with the company for over ten years now. His first popularity depended on a passionate, lyric interpretation of standard ballads and traditional blues, and there was a time when it seemed that Davis might be content with a safe repetition of that formula. But, from time to time, he has undertaken more experimental fare. The *"Kind of Blue"* session of 1959 used highly unorthodox procedures for improvisation and influenced the subsequent development of jazz. And recently, the more exploratory sessions, such as *"E.S.P.," "Miles Smiles,"* and *"Sorcerer,"* have virtually become the rule.

For the work in progress, Miles has augmented his regular quintet with a guitar and has invited pianist Herbie Hancock to try celeste, electronic piano, and electric harpsichord ("I woke up in the middle of the night last night hearing that sound," Miles remarked about the last instrument). One piece already completed for the album is Davis's *Burlena,* which involves the bass and guitar playing one melody line, the horns (Davis and tenor saxophonist Wayne Shorter) another, and drummer Tony Williams improvising an interplaying, percussive third part.

Davis was now in the studio, still chatting with Benson as he picked up and quietly strummed the guitarist's instrument. In the booth, the engineering staff was openly airing its pessimism.

"I kind of knew we wouldn't have to rush into this thing this morning."

"Yeah, I'm sort of surprised *he's* here."

But by 10:05, Davis was in place in the studio, running

down one of the pieces on his horn. Teo Macero, Colum-bia's A & R man, had arrived and was immediately talking on the telephone. Tony Williams and his drums were mak-ing their way through the tangle of mike booms, wires, and baffle boards. And within a few minutes, Wayne Shorter, bassist Ron Carter, and Herbie Hancock had entered, re-moved their coats, taken their places, and were beginning to examine the music on the racks before them.

Macero walked into the studio and embraced Davis. Al-most on his heels arrived orchestrator Gil Evans, a thin, gray, sympathetic, and authoritative presence. "Hey, Gil! You got me some music?" Davis said as a greeting, and the two embraced as Evans answered, "Yes."

"I midwifed a couple of these pieces," Evans continued, referring to the fact that Hancock, Shorter, and Davis wrote most of the numbers to be used, but that he had helped lay a couple of them out for performance.

George Benson was quietly reading and strumming his part. Hancock sat surrounded by his four keyboards, trying out the electric harpsichord. "Which piece shall we work on, Miles?" he asked.

"I don't know," said Davis off-handedly, although he was clearly considering the matter. "Try yours," he said, after a pause—and suddenly Shorter and Davis began phrasing a rolling melody together—a single, casual foot pat from Davis had set the tempo and started them off.

A moment later, Benson and Hancock consulted. "Some of these are chords. Some are just sounds," the pianist-composer explained.

"Hey, Herbie, don't play that one," Davis remarked, in-dicating the harpsichord. "Play the black one," the elec-tronic piano.

Ron Carter, surrounded chest high by baffle boards to isolate the sound of his instrument, surveyed the scene through wire-rimmed glasses, pipe in mouth. Dressed in a dark cardigan sweater, he looked rather like a retired druggist.

As they continued to run down the piece, it became evident that Tony Williams, Davis's young drummer, was feeling his way into it in a highly personal manner. He began with a bit of history, an old-fashioned, regular *ching-de-ching* cymbal beat. By the second or third run-through, he was trying a conservative Latin rhythm, executed chiefly with wire brushes on his snare drum. But within a few more tries, his part had become a complex whirl of cymbal, snare, and tom-tom patterns and accents, although there was no question of where the beat, the basic 1-2-3-4, was falling.

They began on the piece again. Davis counted, "One, two, three, four," but until the music began, he might almost have been tossing off random numbers rather than establishing a strict tempo.

Inside the engineering booth, Macero shuffled through some American Federation of Musicians contracts as he remarked, "That line is hard. It reminds me of those things Miles did for Capitol. Remember them? But this is much freer, of course." He was referring to some recordings by a nine-piece group with Gil Evans, Gerry Mulligan, and others, which started a fad called "cool jazz," and which were imitated in everything from big-band arrangements to cigarette jingles on TV.

Suddenly Davis, whose mike position in the studio had him sitting with his back to the control room, turned and said with a cheerful half-smile, "I want to hear this." In a moment, Macero was reading a complex number, followed by "take one," onto the tape. A run-down of the piece had begun, with Davis and Shorter phrasing together almost as one man.

At the end of a playback Macero got up and, singing and almost dancing his way into the studio, made a quiet point to Davis in the manner of a man telling a casual joke. He was obviously very happy to have started to work.

Davis worked out a couple of bent notes with Ron Carter and then Davis called Gil Evans over to clear up a point in the score, while in the background Carter and Benson ran through a portion of the piece. They were accompanied by impeccable finger-snapping from Tony Williams, who was pacing around the studio, rather like an athlete loosening up after a foot race. By 11:30 the musicians had run through the theme several times more, and it was beginning to swing hard. It was time to take it from the top, including a try at the improvised portions. "Okay, here we go," Davis announced, calling for the intro. "Tony's got two bars."

Halfway through his solo, Davis stopped and turned to Macero, who had reentered the booth. "Hey, Teo, can you make it so it doesn't sound so dull when I hear myself in here? Because what I hear, I don't like."

"I can put a little echo on it, but I'd rather do that when I have more control over it later on."

"Well, if I like it, I can play better."

Macero nodded an unspoken assent, while Laico made an appropriate adjustment among his switches and dials.

A moment later, an engineer entered the studio during the run-through. Davis was highly annoyed and he let Macero know it. During an ensuing pause, Shorter tried out a new reed.

A minute later they were trying the solos again, and Davis was dissatisfied with his background. "Can we change that chord? I don't like that A Minor. Hey, Herbie, play a C

Major." Hancock subjected his C Major to various permutations, interpolating various passing chords along the way. Davis was still dissatisfied. "Play a C chord all through there but put all that other stuff in it," he said tartly.

"Oh, I see what you mean," said Hancock and he tried out the sequence again.

As they ran through Davis's solo, he glanced at the revised chord changes on the music sheet in front of him. And some how he managed to look up at his music from under his eyebrows, although it was well below eye-level.

It was 11:45, and Miles said, "Hey, Teo!"

He was immediately understood. "You want to record this next time." Laico started the tapes rolling.

During the take, Hancock executed a quiet dance with his shoulders, head, and feet as he played; the rest of him was almost immobile. Tony Williams's dance was broader than Hancock's and centered in his elbows. Davis, now satisfied with his chords, did his dancing with his horn.

During the playback, quiet settled on the studio. Macero entered unobtrusively with the income tax withholding forms for the players to fill out, a sure sign that the session was well under way. Davis leaned over a low table, bending from the waist, listening. Shorter munched on a snack he had brought along, but he was listening. As the last notes echoed through the studio, Miles made an inaudible comment, gave Macero a glance that indicated he wanted another take, and then said aloud to his sideman, "Make it tighter."

Hancock: "You want me to stay out of there more?"

Davis: "Yessir!"

Hancock: "But you want me to hit that B-flat chord."

Davis: "Yeah."

Macero (onto the rolling tape): "Take fifteen."

Davis (stopping the take in the middle): "Teo, I sound like I'm playing to the wall."

Macero: "Try it with the earphones on."

They were into another take. Davis, sitting on the edge of his stool, was so involved in his solo that he somehow managed to raise both feet off the ground.

At the end of the take, he looked dissatisfied. But Macero announced, "Martin liked it."

"What the . . . . has Martin got to do with it?"

During the playback, Shorter ducked his head and pulled up his coat collar at something he didn't like in his own solo. But at the end, Davis announced, "That's all right, Teo."

It was 12:30, and by mutual unspoken agreement there was time to try another piece. "This is the one—*Paraphernalia*," said Hancock, selecting a music sheet from the pile in front of him. He turned to the celeste and began running through his part, but after a few of its tinkling notes, Davis asked him to go back to the piano.

There was some discussion of a tricky portion of the piece during which Carter and Hancock are to hold certain chords as long as the soloist wants them, repeat them until the improviser is clearly ready for the next one. Davis sat quietly as the other musicians explained things and worked them out. His presence is authoritative and puts his sidemen on their mettle, and he knows it. But when the moment is right for a decision, he makes one. "Wayne, you don't play the 3/4 bars, and the last 4/4 bar is cut out."

As they ran the piece down, the art of it began to emerge; it didn't sound difficult or complex. Shorter's solo seemed to float, suspended above the rhythm section. For his part, Davis was still instructing as he played. At the end, he crossed to Hancock's keyboard to demonstrate a point, and advised, "It sounds good. But Herbie, don't play all over the piano. Don't go up there," gesturing at the top third of the keyboard. And then he announced to the room in general, "Let's record it. Come on, this is simple."

After a couple of false starts they were into a take. Again Hancock's shoulders danced. During his solo, Davis looked as if half a dozen impressions were attacking his mind at once, but he played as if he were able to condense them all into brief, smoldering, allusive phrases. Shorter built his portion out of ingenious fragments of the main theme. Hancock echoed the theme in his section too, but quite differently. During Tony Williams's spot, Davis's expression showed his approval, and he signaled to Benson to take a solo as the tape was still rolling.

"Let's hear some of that, Teo," Miles requested at the end. As the playback began to fill the studio, he executed a quick sideways step across the floor in time to the music, then paused and said quietly, "That's hard work—making records." (*1969*)

III

Annotations

A prominent American musician once described record annotations ("liner notes" to those in the trade) as one of the more dubious forms of music journalism. There can be no doubt that for jazz LPs, the practice of writing notes has produced more than its share of puffery and ephemera. Yet future scholars of American music may also find in record notes insights into many an artist's aspirations and intentions, sometimes valuable interviews—in short, important bits of history—and (on occasion) some enlightening musical comment and analysis. It is with the hope that the reader may discover some of the latter in them that the notes which follow are included here.

ॐ

THE IMMORTAL
JELLY ROLL MORTON

(Milestone MLP 2003 included early Morton material from the Paramount, Autograph, and Rialto labels
recorded between 1923 and 1925. Those selections, plus
the classic 1923-24 Gennett piano solos, *King Porter,
New Orleans Blues, Grandpa's Spells, Kansas City
Stomps, The Pearls,* etc., were later included in the
two-disc Milestone set M-47018. Excellent, updated LP
transfers of the piano solos appeared briefly on the collectors' label Fountain FJ 104.)

Anyone who is not familiar with the music on this LP is of
course invited to dig in herewith. And so is anyone who is
familiar with it, for he may get some surprises. For the tape
and LP transfer of these venerable recordings has been accomplished with cleanness and clarity. Milestone began
with clear copies of the originals and then carefully dubbed
and filtered them with no sacrifice of musical values. So listen. You may hear things you never heard before from Jelly
Roll Morton.

Now nobody is attempting a con job. There is a bit of
outright trivia here, and there are a couple of failures—interesting failures, to be sure. However, there are two fine
band sides; there are at least three excellent Morton piano
solos on three of his best pieces; there is a very good duet;
there is a sketch or two for important later work; and there
are several very good moments on some of the other selections. That, it seems to me, is a great deal to get from
any LP.

We begin (to put things in strict historical order for the moment) where Ferdinand "Jelly Roll" Morton, the diamond-toothed dandy from New Orleans, first began in the recording studios as far as we know, with the 1923 band recording of *Big Fat Ham* and *Muddy Water Blues*. No doubt it was a case of Morton, the musical braggart, backing up the things he had been telling Chicago about how good he was. And we carry him through his second recorded experiment with the juxtaposition of piano and clarinet on *Wolverine Blues* (1925), a practice and a piece he was to return to later. (You can hear the very first such juxtaposition briefly on this version of *Mr. Jelly Lord*.)

Mamanita—the title is actually *Mama 'Nita,* for Anita, and no doubt for Anita Gonzales (those seeking further information should consult Alan Lomax's biography of Morton, *Mister Jelly Roll*). The piece is one of Morton's best jazz tangos, and this is easily the best version of it, lively, bright and rhythmically inventive in a way that belies its date. Indeed some of those marvelously tantalizing behind-the-beat things that Morton impossibly gets into, and so cleanly and neatly gets out of, might be the envy and delight of any jazz pianist of any era.

Most people who know about Morton's music may know the remarkable story of how the *Froggy Moore* solo was rescued by John Steiner from a Chicago junk shop in the mid-1950s, as a blank, unidentified test-pressing of a commercially unissued recording which turned out to be Jelly Roll Morton playing one of his best pieces.

The piece was variously known as *Froggy Moore, Frog-i-More Rag,* and, when words were put to its third theme, *Sweetheart o' Mine*. It was once said to have been named for a stage contortionist named Moore whom Morton had accompanied in California; it seems he wore a frog costume during his act. Thornton Hagert subsequently discovered evidence of a pianist called "Frog Eye" Moore from whom Morton probably borrowed the piece's intriguing, tonally ambiguous introduction.

Critic-composer William Russell has commented on the two final choruses here, the trio theme and Morton's rocking variation on it:

> The beautiful chorale-like melody of the *Frog-i-More* trio is first played very simply, in a style reminiscent of the sustained trio of *Wolverine Blues*. This first . . . "organ chorus" . . . is played entirely in the treble range. On paper the tune, with its constantly repeated motive, presents a singularly four-square appearance, but Jelly's performance is a revelation of rhythmic variety by means of such devices as shifted accents, slight delays, and anticipations. . . .
>
> "The real marvel . . . is the final trio chorus . . . The melodic invention of this finale is as notable as its immense rhythmic vitality. Although the melodic developments of the stomp version follow closely the simple lines of the "organ chorus," Jelly's rhythmic impetus and melodic embellishment give the effect of fantastic and frenzied variation. Actually each bar is directly related to its counterpart in the first simple statement, and all of Jelly's most characteristic and fanciful "figurations" are fused with the basic idea as though they belonged there originally . . . But with Jelly Roll, no matter how exuberant rhythmically or varied melodically the final choruses become, there never is any doubt of their musical logic and that each note grows out of the original motive.

London Blues proved to be one of Morton's most durable pieces. Rivaling *King Porter Stomp* and *Wolverine Blues* for longevity, it was recorded in 1923 by King Oliver and in 1938 by a Lionel Hampton group under its better-known title, *Shoe Shiner's Drag*. For the lay listener, the piece is made particularly intriguing by the "breaks," the various momentary two-bar suspensions of the beat, that come in pairs at the beginnings of the choruses. Good breaks were a cornerstone of jazz to Morton, of course. (These contrast nicely with the wonderful breaks on *Big Fat Ham,* which terminate phrases and choruses.) For musicians, however, *London Blues* has an interesting set of substitute blues chord changes in its main theme; these become even more fascinating when you emphasize that this was recorded in 1923, and might have been conceived who-knows-how-many-years before that. Also note Morton's darting left hand in his next-to-last chorus, and, by contrast, his right hand in his last chorus.

Good structure was one of Morton's primary musical concerns. Take, for example, the various uses the main "trio" theme of *Wolverine Blues* is put to here, and the overall pattern that lies behind them. Actually most of this version is based on the trio except for Morton's solo. (*Wolverine,* of course, is not a twelve-bar blues.) Or hear Morton's piano part on *Mr. Jelly Lord.* No matter what sort of irreverent hokum may otherwise be going on, Jelly Roll himself builds his part both spontaneously and thoughtfully.

As I have indicated above, *Big Fat Ham* (later *Ham and Eggs*) and *Muddy Water Blues* made an auspicious beginning on records for Morton, and they rank with the best of his band recordings—which means with his 1926-28 Victors. They are therefore almost a summary of everything that New Orleans jazz had achieved before the arrival of Louis Armstrong. Appropriately, their primary quality is their nearly perfect rhythmic cohesion. Would that we knew who the Keppard-like cornetist is, for he rivals George Mitchell as an interpreter of Morton, both for his poised and easy energy on *Ham* and his soulful playing on *Muddy Water.* (And don't miss Morton's almost wild accompaniment to the cornetist's solo on the latter.) Jasper Taylor plays wood blocks here, not necessarily because he played them on the job, but because snare drums, bass drum, and cymbals wouldn't register on the early recording equipment. Taylor also seems ideal rhythmically for Jelly's music. And please note that Morton uses both clarinet and alto sax in the polyphonic ensembles here, and uses them carefully and well.

Fish Tail Blues and *High Society* have their problems, to be sure (not the least of which is Alex Poole's inability to swing), but the former is a sketch for one of Jelly Roll's best-known Victor records, *Sidewalk Blues*. In *Evergreen Review #35*, Lee Collins reminisced about this date in an excerpt from his autobiography:

> I tell you, he was some character! . . . "You know that you will be working with the world's greatest jazz piano player," he boasted. I told him I knew he was one of the greatest jazz pianists, but he said, "Not one of the greatest—I am the greatest!"
>
> We went . . . to see the manager of a big name ballroom out on the South Side. But he and this man could not come to any agreement on the price Jelly wanted for playing there.
>
> Jelly told the manager, "You bring Paul Whiteman out here and pay any price he wants because he has the name of 'king of jazz.' But you happen to be talking to the real king of jazz. I invented it and I brought it here."
>
> Jelly and I did make some recordings on the Autograph label. We made *High Society, Weary Blues, Tiger Rag,* and *Fish Tail Blues.* The last number was mine but I never received any credit for it. Roy Palmer, the trombonist, warned me not to play it until I had it copyrighted but I did not take his advice.
>
> The clarinet player on those records was an old fellow named Ball, "Balls Ball," as he was known. I never heard of him before we made those records and never saw him again afterwards . . . but he played *High Society*, so I think he must have come from New Orleans originally.

As I say, there are some failures here and there are some curiosities, but *Mamanita, Froggy Moore, London Blues, Wolverine Blues, Big Fat Ham, Muddy Water*—they announced a major composer, performer, and band leader. And they carry their years beautifully.

ह्ब

THE IMMORTAL KING OLIVER

(The Oliver album on Milestone MLP 2006 collected two duets by King Oliver and Jelly Roll Morton, three titles by the Oliver Creole Jazz Band with Louis Armstrong in a total of five "takes," three selections by small Clarence Williams groups that had Oliver's cornet, and the Oliver accompaniments to Sara Martin, including the singular *Death Sting Me*. The Morton duets and the Creole Jazz Band selections were subsequently included in the Milestone two-record set M-47017 *"Louis Armstrong and King Oliver."*)

King Oliver's Creole Jazz Band, as the faithful do not need to be reminded, was one of the most celebrated ensembles in jazz history. This LP reveals the artistry of that group and the talents of its leader as no other collection ever has.

It was not simply the presence of the young Louis Armstrong that made Oliver's ensemble so celebrated, by the way. Clarinetist Garvin Bushell has spoken of his reaction to hearing the Oliver group in Chicago in 1921, before Armstrong joined it, while he and trumpeter Bubber Miley were touring with Mamie Smith.

. . . I was very much impressed with their blues and with their sound. The trumpets and clarinets in the East had a

better 'legitimate' quality, but their sound touched you
more. It was less cultivated but more expressive of how the
people felt. Bubber and I sat there with our mouths open.

We talked with the Dodds brothers. They felt very highly
about what they were playing as though they knew they
were doing something new that nobody else could do. I'd
say they did regard themselves as artists, in the sense we use
the term today.*

Armstrong has declared that Oliver was a major influence; and, through Bubber Miley, Oliver's work had a for-
mative effect on young Duke Ellington. Therefore whatever
enables us to get to know Oliver better is valuable historically. It is also valuable in and of itself.

The Creole Band recorded for four different labels. Paramount, the source of these titles, was the last of them, and
the Paramount titles are pivotal.

Nothing gets us inside a jazz performance and acquaints
us more deeply with the nature of jazz improvisation so
much as comparisons—comparisons not necessarily of two
groups playing the same piece, but of the same group playing the same piece. Better still, the same group playing the
piece successively on the same occasion! And in the Paramount sessions, not only did the Oliver Band duplicate titles
recorded for other labels (*Mabel's Dream, Riverside Blues*),
but Paramount policy resulted, for *Mabel's Dream* and
Southern Stomps, in the release of invaluable alternate
"takes" made at the same session.

Although the Creole Band's records reveal a great deal
about Oliver, they do not reveal all. The rest of the program
on this LP—with Oliver in duet with Jelly Roll Morton,
Oliver as featured soloist with Clarence Williams's small

* From "Jazz in the Twenties: Garvin Bushell" by Nat Hentoff in *Jazz
Panorama* (da Capo).

groups, and Oliver as blues accompanist—reveals other aspects of his art.

The Morton duets are on the pianist's most famous piece, *King Porter Stomp,* and his *Tom Cat Blues,* a piece Morton also titled *Midnight Mama* on occasion—and to be entirely esoteric about the matter, it is a splicing of themes otherwise called *Mecca Flat Blues* or *Nobody Knows the Way I Feel This Morning* and *Whinin' Boy Blues.*

In Alan Lomax's *Mister Jelly Roll,* Morton remembered Oliver's prowess on this session, particularly the way he picked up the tunes after just a run-through. On *King Porter* we can hear evidence of the great power for which the younger Oliver had been noted. That power had diminished by 1924 to be sure, but the soul—Oliver's singular paradox of dignified anguish and joy—is there, and is unforgettable once one has experienced it. It is wonderful to hear Oliver play these figurations (as Morton called them) on King Porter's main theme, variations which were shortly to influence swing band arranging so pervasively. The opening of *Tom Cat* is notable for the variety of muted sounds which Oliver employs. And its ending for Oliver's versions of ideas which obviously impressed the young Armstrong deeply.

To return to the Creole Band, the initial take of *Mabel's Dream,* which fades up rapidly in its first couple of bars, has never before been on LP, and it makes an interesting comparison to the more familiar, more jaunty second take in several respects. Probably the most important respect is in the statement and variations on the final theme in which Oliver's horn has the lead. Although each of these Oliver "solos" is different, each uses basically the same plan. Taking the theme as his point of departure, Oliver gradually interpolates blues fragments, and, following through, builds each of these in turn into a variant theme. Each time, the fragments are different and each time, they therefore lead him to a different conclusion. Oliver, the passionate cornetist, was also a thoughtful and logical improviser. And above all, and always, he was a melodist.

The first take of the swinging *Southern Stomps* has not been issued since its initial appearance in 1923. For this LP, Oliver expert Walter C. Allen lent his copy of the original. I prefer it to the more familiar version; Armstrong's lead in the opening ensemble seems more inventive to me, for one thing. We have different clarinet breaks by Johnny Dodds. And here is concrete evidence of one of the most fabled and celebrated practices of the Creole Band in its nightly appearances at Chicago's Lincoln Gardens—entirely different, spontaneous, two-cornet breaks by Oliver and Armstrong on different performances of the same piece.

Finally, *Riverside Blues:* it would be a gem if only for the magnificent interplay of Oliver and Armstrong in the final two choruses, after Dodds and Dutrey have each soloed over modified stop-time. It is Oliver who leads the ensemble for the first twelve-measure chorus. Armstrong takes over in solo for eight. Then Oliver comes in for four more. But when both men are playing, there is a fascinating interplay of each with the other.

The three Clarence Williams titles included here are those for which there is now general agreement that Oliver is the cornet soloist. Thus, *Bozo* has solos by trombonist Ed Cuffee, by Oliver in wa-wa style, plus a musicianly clarinet solo by Bennie Moten (he was not, of course, the Kansas City bandleader), and a loose, New Orleans-style ensemble on the out chorus, with Cy St. Clair's mobile tuba much in evidence throughout.

On the Charleston-style *Bimbo,* there is a full chorus by Oliver on open horn, but with an almost muted edge to his sound, plus a later Oliver half-chorus. And on *Speakeasy,* the cornetist's plaintive open horn sets the tone of the performance after the intro.

The singular blues recording *Death Sting Me* would undoubtedly be a classic only for its arresting lyric. Sara Martin, a prolific recording artist in the 1920s, delivers it with somewhat "formal" diction but full sincerity. The performance is more than adorned by Oliver's expressive introduction and interplaying comments. *Mistreatin' Man* has a more formal arrangement, and besides Oliver's muted work, some appealingly robust comments from a trombonist most of the references now identify as Charlie Green. *Mean, Tight Mama* calls for a new element of cajoling, mocking humor, and Oliver provides it excellently.

To end this on a personal note, I have been listening to Oliver's music, and to some of these very recordings, for over twenty-five years, and yet on no occasion do I return to it without the rewards of discovering something new in it. In playing the music to prepare these comments, my rewards have been many and great.   (*1968*)

CUTTIN' THE BOOGIE

(The New World records anthology [NW 259] of "piano blues and boogie woogie"—to give its subtitle— collected sixteen boogie-woogie selections by a total of eight pianists. Its notes included a brief opening essay followed by individual comments on the performances. I have here omitted the technical and discographical details that accompanied the latter.)

In the spring of 1940, the big swing band of drummer Will Bradley had its first hit, a two-sided 78 rpm disc called *Beat Me, Daddy, Eight to the Bar*. Bradley soon followed with *Scrub Me, Mamma, with a Boogie Beat* (adapted from *The Irish Washerwoman*). And with World War II mobilization came *Boogie Woogie Bugle Boy* by the Andrews Sisters.

Through such amiable but hardly authentic ditties boogie-woogie entered the consciousness of millions. Such numbers helped keep the swing bands popular. And soon everyone was learning a slew-footed, hip-wriggling dance to go with boogie-woogie.

In the first half of the forties, every dance band (whether a real swing band or not), every small group, every solo pianist had to have at least one boogie-woogie number—or, if not, had to call something "boogie" whether it really was or not. And composer Morton Gould wrote, and pianist José Iturbi recorded, "Boogie Woogie Étude." Because neither man understood the polyrhythms that give the style its vitality, the record is rather embarrassing.

Fortunately, there was also more serious and more authentic work. An idiom like boogie-woogie, and the adaptation of it to a big swing band, can't be merely the work of songwriters or of the average hack arrangers. By mid-1937 pianist and composer Mary Lou Williams had recorded her boogie *Overhand* as a piano solo and had scored her *Roll 'Em*, for the Benny Goodman band. She then did *Little Joe from Chicago* for the successful ensemble that was her home base, Andy Kirk's orchestra. By 1938 the Bob Crosby orchestra had both *Yancey Special* and *Honky Tonk Train* in its book, and the Tommy Dorsey band had an arrangement by Dean Kincaide of *Boogie Woogie*. A couple of years later the less prominent Teddy Powell band offered Bob Mersey's scoring of *Boogin' on the Downbeat*.

But even with that kind of activity there needs to be a

more creative source of inspiration supplying the music. There was.

The key lies in the composer credits on the highly successful Dorsey disc to "Pinetop" Smith, on the two Crosby recordings to Meade "Lux" Lewis, and on the Powell to Pete Johnson (*Boogin' on the Downbeat* was adapted from his *Blues on the Downbeat*).

These men and a few others—all pianists—were the composer-improvisers from whose splendid, unpretentious work all else derived. And they were also the able carriers of a tradition that is older than anyone knows.

Boogie-woogie is basically a way of playing the twelve-bar blues on a piano. The Afro-American blues is a story in itself and a large one, since it is the only musical form created in the United States, accounts for so much of our music by now, and is international as well, readily understood by musicians in Tokyo and Liverpool, Paris and Johannesburg.

Boogie-woogie is a highly percussive style in which the left hand plays a sustained bass figure, usually of one or two measures, usually with eight beats to the bar. Over that continuous pattern the right hand improvises percussive figures that interplay in fascinating and varied polyrhythmic, polymetric patterns. The right hand basically "thinks" in $4/4$, however, with all four beats usually given equal value, and a drummer accompanying a boogie pianist would ordinarily play in four, not eight.

Just as we don't know where the blues came from, or when, we don't know where boogie-woogie came from, or when. It is often said that ragtime developed as a somewhat middle-class and European-oriented music because it takes a piano to play ragtime, and it takes money to buy a piano. True, but it also takes a piano to play boogie-woogie, and boogie-woogie is obviously less European in its orientation than ragtime.

Boogie-woogie seems to have been a midwestern style, heard early in urban and rural Texas, Oklahoma, and Missouri in barrooms and mining camps, honky-tonks and lumber camps. Indeed, according to Jelly Roll Morton's reminiscences recorded for the Library of Congress, a boogie-woogie-like piano blues style had already been heard in New Orleans by the turn of the century.

By the time the boogie-woogie idiom got recorded it was already relatively sure and well defined under the hands of its best players. One of the first to record in the style, or something near it, was Fletcher Henderson, who used an intermittent walking bass (a technique that also appears briefly in some ragtime pieces) in his 1923 *Chimes Blues,* as did one Clay Custer in *The Rocks* the same year. (Hear a piece like Jimmy Blythe's *Chicago Blues,* discussed below, for the best explanation of the term "walking bass.") But Henderson had destinies other than blues piano—the development of the big band and the foundation of the swing era itself. Custer dropped into obscurity.

We do know about James Blythe and his associates, however, and around him and them developed what came to be 1930s' boogie-woogie. In 1916, when he was about fifteen, Blythe moved from Louisville to Chicago, which later became a center for the piano blues and its recording. Blythe was a kind of house pianist at Paramount Records, leading little blues groups of various sizes and instrumentations, working with singers, and recording a few piano solos of his own. At night in the bars around the South Side and at rent parties his piano associates included two younger Chicagoans, Meade "Lux" Lewis and Albert Ammons; a somewhat older player, Jimmy Yancey; Clarence "Pinetop" Smith, from Alabama; Hersal Thomas, from Texas; "Cripple" Clarence Lofton; and J. H. "Mr. Freddie" Shayne.

Blythe, Thomas, and Shayne were the professional players. Yancey and Lofton were gifted semipros. Lewis and Ammons were the strong younger professionals-to-be who were to help carry the music into its widespread public revival. Smith would have, too, had he not been killed at twenty-five by a stray bullet, an innocent bystander at someone else's fight.

By the thirties Lewis and Ammons had been joined by a pianist from Kansas City, Pete Johnson, and for a while by Johnson's Kansas City associate, the masterful blues singer Joe Turner.

Lewis had recorded *Honky Tonk Train* for Paramount in 1927, and John Hammond, the jazz entrepreneur and record producer, eventually heard it. Given the opportunity to make some jazz records for Parlophone, a British firm (the American labels weren't recording enough jazz for Parlophone's markets), Hammond found Lewis working in a Chicago car-wash and had him re-record the piece in 1935. He then encouraged Benny Goodman to invite Lewis, Ammons, and Johnson to guest on Goodman's radio broadcasts. As the Boogie-Woogie Trio they had long stays at a Greenwich Village nightclub with a slightly ironic name, Café Society, and at Chicago's Hotel Sherman. They made records. An affluent, nightclubbing middle class was discovering the real thing, which most of the buyers of the Will Bradley *Beat Me, Daddy* probably never got around to hearing.

The boogie-woogie craze had its day, and that day was largely over by the early fifties. But what about the style? In the rhythm and blues and rock 'n' roll of the fifties and sixties, boogie bass lines were everywhere, particularly the bass you'll hear here on *Yancey Special*. Indeed, in the mid-sixties a pianist named Roy Meriweather had a hit with something called *Cow Cow Boogaloo,* an almost note-for-note rendering of a twenties' boogie record of Charles "Cow Cow" Davenport.

Devices stemming directly or indirectly from boogie-woogie still permeate rock and pop music. In one popular survival, to our country-and-western bands "playing a boogie" means laying down a traditional boogie-woogie bass line, usually on guitar or bass guitar and usually under a twelve-bar blues.

In their forties' work, Lewis and Johnson particularly went on to develop some innovative techniques. In Lewis's five-minute *Bass on Top,* for example, his walking-bass left hand moves up the keyboard through his treble figures and back again. Johnson's breakneck *Holler Stomp* has a bass line in a kind of half-walk and in its virtuoso middle choruses abandons the ordinarily percussive character of boogie for a flowing eight-measure line. Johnson's fine slow blues, *You Don't Know My Mind,* should also be mentioned, and Ammons's delightful extended rendering of Hersal Thomas's *Suitcase Blues.*

One word of caution: Music like this, which works within very limited stylistic means, creates difficulties for LP programming. Three-minute performances, eight selections at a time, may make listening problems if the album is just put on the turntable and let go. Better perhaps to take the music in small doses at first, maybe one pianist at a time. Then the commendable variety that each of these players achieved within this very limited form and style will become even more of a revelation and delight.

Recordings

Jimmy Blythe's musical leadership among Chicago piano bluesmen will be obvious to anyone familiar with the later work of Ammons and Lewis. In *Chicago Stomp* (1924) and *Armour Avenue Struggle,* he spelled out his importance clearly on his first solo recordings.

Chicago Stomp is deceptive, for what starts out as an apparently regular walking bass is varied so often and enunciated so differently (compare the first chorus with the second, for example) that simply following Blythe's left hand can become interesting in itself. But one's recognition of Blythe's obvious musicianship should not obscure the appreciation of the sprightly spontaneous character of his playing.

Blythe's treatment of J. H. Shayne's *Mr. Freddie Blues* (1926) is intermittently a boogie-woogie performance and a straight blues without the boogie bass line. It is very easy for a performer to lose momentum and fullness using that approach, particularly at moments when the boogie bass is dropped. But Blythe (unlike some later players who tried the idea—hear Pete Johnson's *Pete's Mixture,* for example) does not.

Shayne's piece is basically a one-chorus idea, and part of the interest here comes from following the variations through which Blythe explores that idea thematically.

Hersal Thomas's *Suitcase Blues* (1925) probably should not be called true boogie-woogie. It offers two basic chorus ideas. One is played over a simple, heavy blues bass of four even accents. The other is played over growling, rumbling slides—an idea that in itself might entitle a player to some kind of immortality. Thomas, a piano prodigy in his childhood, died from poisoning while in his teens and soon after his few recordings were made.

Clarence "Pinetop" Smith's *Pinetop's Boogie Woogie* (1928) is the piece that gave the style its name and became one of its most imitated and influential recordings.

The title seems almost an accident: in an alternate take,

Smith, in his running instructions to listeners, dancers, and the "gal with the red dress on," calls it "Pinetop's Truck." "Truck" (which later gave its name to the thirties dance) is a southernism for "mess" or "stuff" or "to-do," a kind of modest, mocking self-disparagement, utterly serious under the surface, and very appropriate to the ironic emotional language of the blues.

Paul Oliver suggested that the term "boogie-woogie" may have derived from "booger-rooger," a party or celebration, and in the early thirties "pitchin' boogie" did come to mean throwing a party. But one characteristic of any slang vernacular is that the meaning and currency of its expressions are in constant flux.

Pinetop's piece, with its three basic chorus ideas (one of them actually a simple vamp) and its tantalizingly easy two-bar break ("Hold it now! Stop!"), is a gem of composition and performance. Its effectiveness clearly centers on the compelling buoyancy of Smith's touch and the crystal clarity of his articulation in each hand.

Jump Steady Blues (1929) is Pinetop Smith's only true solo performance.

In the early twenties it was common to call all boogie-woogie bass figures "rocks," but gradually the term began to be applied to the kind of one-measure figure heard in the previous piece to differentiate it from the two-measure walking bass heard here. Yet Smith's walking bass, rather like Blythe's in *Chicago Stomp*, is resolved at the end of each chorus along with his treble. Again, one of his treble ideas is basically a timekeeping, offbeat vamp, but notice how differently it is articulated here. And again, Pinetop's clarity and easy touch—the despair of all his imitators—is the central virtue around which all the others gather.

The 1935 Parlophone version of the *Honky Tonk Train* was Lewis's second (and least-known) version of his masterpiece in the long-standing tradition of the descriptive "train blues." In his essay in *Jazzmen,* William Russell wrote of it that:

> Lewis's ideas seem unlimited; in developing them he always gives an unexpected twist to the melody. A new technical idea is used for each chorus; one composed of high tremolos and repeated chords is followed by a variation based on light glissandi, and that in turn by one strongly rhythmic, with heavy bass figures for contrast. Dynamic variety and cross-rhythms have been employed to a much greater extent by Meade Lux than by any other pianist. From the drive and complexity of rhythm one might imagine that the *Honky Tonk Train Blues* was played by two pianists. . . . The recurring bass figure does not suggest monotony or lack of invention, but holds the listener. In common with other self-taught pianists of this school, Meade Lux does not use the damper or any other pedal, except to strike with his foot for the percussive effect.

Incidentally, the striking double-time "train-crossing-the-trestle" effect in the sixth chorus proved too difficult for most pianists who undertook *Honky Tonk Train* in the thirties and forties, and they omitted it.

Once he was established with his public, Lewis tended to feel boxed in by the boogie-woogie style and by this piece. Although self-taught, he was a skillful pianist and wanted to play things other than blues. (On one of his thirties' records he performs *I'm in the Mood for Love* on celeste.) He lamentably responded to nightly requests for *Honky Tonk Train* by performing it faster and faster over the years.

As Russell points out, two ways Lewis gives interest to *Honky Tonk Train* are by using only the white keys in his bass line, although the piece is in G, and avoiding the tonic until the end. That ending, by the way, does not here employ the resolving tremolo that appears in all his other recorded versions.

Lewis's direct debt to Jimmy Yancey first showed up on his 1930 recordings as accompanist to singer George Hannah in *Freakish Blues*. On his 1936 *Yancey Special* the debt is heard in a fully developed statement (but, as William Russell observed in *Jazzmen*, an almost sedate one), with that quality of compositional completeness that Lewis so often gave his extemporizations. The bass figure can be found in Yancey, of course, but, so far as I have been able to discover, *without* the octave that Lewis gives it. As in *Honky Tonk Train* (and in many other boogie-woogie pieces), Lewis tends to end each chorus with a version of the same four measures. But notice the opening: with no introduction, he offers eight measures of bass, unexpectedly ending the chorus with two hands playing the identifying four measures. And notice also the bass's relationship to several of the treble motives he introduces.

Lewis's 1936 treatment of the Shayne *Mr. Freddie Blues* is both similar to and in striking contrast to Blythe's. Lewis plays in sustained boogie style throughout, and although he uses the *Mr. Freddie* one-chorus idea as the basis of much of what he does—it even determines his introduction—his treatment of it reaches further and is looser and more varied. A detailed comparison of the two versions might serve as a fascinating exposition of Lewis's contribution to the boogie-woogie idiom.

Albert Ammons's most personal performance is probably his *Shout for Joy*. But a great deal of his work offered a personal restatement and refinement of the music of earlier players.

As Ammons himself acknowledged, *Boogie Woogie Stomp* (1936) is clearly a reinterpretation of *Pinetop's Boogie*

Woogie. Ammons substitutes his own power and drive for Smith's buoyancy and delicacy, and the remarkable thing is that it works.

In *Bass Goin' Crazy* (1939) Ammons pays tribute to such predecessors as Charles "Cow Cow" Davenport and "Cripple" Clarence Lofton. Those men (Lofton particularly) are sometimes said to have played boogie-woogie blues in a kind of intuitive free form in which a chorus of fourteen measures might be followed by one of eleven and a half. They also tended to play with clipped, ragtime-like accents, played eight-to-the-bar patterns in both hands for long stretches, and switched bass figures with what seems near-abandon. Ammons has here patterned and regularized their ideas and made them swing in a piece with a spontaneity of its own, and with a bass that is a lot less "crazy" than it may seem at first.

Jimmy Yancey had never recorded until 1939, and he was recorded then because of the tribute in Meade Lewis's title *Yancey Special* and the interest in him that it stimulated.

Yancey defies all the rules. He was a rudimentary pianist in several senses, yet his work is rhythmically fascinating, and for most listeners he has the sensibilities and depth of a true artist. *The Mellow Blues,* variations on a kind of broken Charleston rhythm, has a couple of howling mistakes (the end of the third chorus, for example). It is a two-part improvisation, with Yancey's bass line possibly even more spontaneously interesting than his treble. His overall pacing is commendable, and a very Pinetop-like calm chorus (the fifth) comes at precisely the right moment. As a youngster, Yancy had worked in vaudeville as a dancer, and surely the experience affected his piano-playing style.

The title of Yancey's *Tell 'Em About Me* (1939) is from the blues verse "If you get to Chicago [or wherever], won't you tell 'em about me." The performance is the most lyrical of all Yancey's blues. In his essay "Boogie Woogie," William Russell considers it one of Yancey's earliest pieces and says, "Yancey's ability to hold his composition together and keep it moving and rocking with such sparseness of notes is astonishing."

To add further to the wonderful contradictions that were Jimmy Yancey: in February 1930, Henry Brown, born in Tennessee, raised in St. Louis, recorded *Deep Morgan* in a style similar to Yancey's.

If Yancey's similar abrupt endings to his performances puzzle the listener—well, it was the only ending he knew.

Climbin' and Screamin' (1939) is the best of several solo versions which Pete Johnson recorded of his obviously favorite piece, the one he also used as the basis of his famous duo performance with singer Joe Turner, *Roll 'Em, Pete*. Johnson probably had more swing than any other boogie man with the possible exception of Smith, and that swing was undoubtedly the result of his musical upbringing in Kansas City. His work has the triplet feel, derived from Louis Armstrong's jazz innovations, that is shared by the best players from that city's musical maturity, up through Charlie Parker. Johnson directly influenced such fifties "funky" players as Horace Silver, Ray Bryant, and Junior Mance. And as pianist Nat Pierce has remarked, to keep up this kind of momentum the forearm and wrist have to be rigid but loose at the same time, a quality probably more evident in Johnson's work than in that of any other pianist in this collection. Johnson was a master at building up his right hand effects with short percussive one- or two-measure riffs, but he could also connect these ideas into flowing phrases of several measures, as his opening choruses here ably demonstrate.

Blues on the Downbeat (1940), in one of Johnson's strongest and most polished recordings, uses his second-favorite

bass figure. His mid-performance break, in which he tantalizingly drops and then resumes his bass, is handled with
such originality and is such a fine example of suspension,
tension, and release that it is a pity he did not use the device
more often. Johnson also seems to use the familiar pattern
of concluding each chorus with the same four-measure ending, but here there are hidden variants on that ending to be
heard here.

Johnson's *Kaycee on My Mind* (1940) is a masterpiece of
sustained rocking swing and the kind of performance that
probably had no preconceptions before it was recorded except a tempo, a bass figure, and a mood. Notice the loose
asymmetry of Johnson's treble accents in the opening of the
second chorus. The switch to a walking bass for the last two
choruses was typical of a Johnson performance, and here he
makes it work. The combination of momentum, introspection, melancholy, and good cheer is also typical of the pur-
gative irony of all good blues performances.

In the Boogie Woogie Trio of Lewis, Ammons, and Johnson, solo space was left for each man. With Meade "Lux"
Lewis's departure, however, the Ammons and Johnson duo
tended to improvise simultaneously throughout each performance, with delightful rhythmic results. *Cuttin' the Boogie*
(apparently built on Johnson's *Basement Boogie*) probably
shows their contrapuntal interplay with more clarity than
any other of their recordings. It remains for the listener, by
this point enlightened in the characteristics of each pianist's
style, to follow the fine game of deciding who is playing
what on *Cuttin' the Boogie*. (*1977*)

ᘒᕗ

BENNY CARTER
Further Definitions

(The LP discussed below was first issued as Impulse album S-12. *Further Definitions* has subsequently appeared as MCA 29009. The 1930s French Swing recordings, with Carter, Coleman Hawkins, and Django Reinhardt, which inspired the album, were last issued in the U.S. as Prestige S-7633. They may also be available on French import issues.)

The longer we live, the saying goes, the more we are convinced that the great reputations are deserved. The truly great reputations on alto saxophone in jazz have belonged to Benny Carter, Johnny Hodges, and the late Charlie Parker. And possibly because he has had fewer direct imitators, Carter's real originality shines forth perhaps most boldly of the three. Jazzmen who number him among the great alto players include Erroll Garner, Pete Rugolo, Lester Young, J. J. Johnson, Dizzy Gillespie, and Louis Armstrong. But Carter's reputation does not depend only on the alto, for he has been an outstanding jazz composer-arranger and trumpet soloist as well. Miles Davis (who regularly plays Carter's piece *When Lights Are Low,* by the way) has attested that Carter is a whole musical education in himself. And Cannonball Adderley has written of him that "he was one of the first virtuosi . . . but he makes it look so easy."

Carter has done some jazz recording lately and written a lot for the Count Basie orchestra, but much of his time has been spent scoring for television (*M-Squad,* for example), for movies (*Flower Drum Song,* for example) and for several singers (Dakota Staton, for example). This LP announces his intention to be more active as a jazz player from now on. And, as we shall see, it contains succinct examples of his ability as an arranger as well.

The recital also reunites Benny Carter with Coleman Hawkins. Hawkins, as I probably do not need to remark, was and is one of *the* tenor saxophonists in jazz, and perhaps the first to develop a really authentic jazz style on his instrument. And, like Carter, he is the kind of player whose best work never becomes dated.

In 1937 (on April 28th, to be exact) Hawkins and Carter recorded together in Paris, *Crazy Rhythm* and *Honeysuckle Rose,* and both performances became classics for both men. The instrumentation here is exactly the same as it was on those original sides: four saxes, four rhythm (piano, bass, drums, and guitarist Django Reinhardt on the Paris date).

The sessions that went into making this LP were particularly happy and were well-attended by visitors. Coleman Hawkins, by the way, arrived for one session in his working uniform of black tie and tux, swearing that he had not just come from last night's gig, but was already prepared for tonight's. Hawkins seemed especially glad to be able to tell visiting Buster Bailey, who was a fellow member with both Hawkins and Carter of the Fletcher Henderson orchestra, that Carter wanted to return to more active life as a player. Participant Charlie Rouse, when complimented on the exciting way that things were going, beamed that "we are all so happy to be playing with Benny."

Phil Woods, one of the comparative youngsters in this company, read these charts with a beautiful understanding and sympathy; he seemed to recognize their musical meaning immediately. Woods made the suggestion that the rhythm play doubletime on *Blue Star,* during Carter's outstanding section writing toward the end of that piece.

Otherwise, as he said (and as you can hear), those sax variations would sound like dance-band ballad playing, and they are far more than that. Woods's own style has become very individual and, to me, it now reflects a selective knowledge of the jazz of the thirties as well as of his own generation (hear him on *Crazy Rhythm,* for instance).

Bassist Jimmy Garrison's fine exuberance can be felt immediately on hearing this music. Garrison has worked with a variety of players, including Lennie Tristano, Kenny Dorham, Bill Evans, and more recently, Ornette Coleman. Here he somehow reminds me of a cross between Pops Foster and Percy Heath—and that is a compliment to all three of them.

Quickness of mind is one of the first and most exciting aspects of Carter's playing. And it is, for me, one of the outstanding qualities of pianist Dick Katz. Katz is the kind of player who has sound judgment and taste about what is really artistic, and what is merely fashionable, in the jazz tradition. One can hear his quick receptive feeling for Carter and Hawkins constantly here—in the fleet, discreet response with which he complements phrase after phrase in the writing and by the soloists. Katz is also one of those players who has developed the capacity to swing with real musical ideas with almost understated quietness and delicacy. And his solo on *Cotton Tail* has a humor (watch that subtly appropriate excursion into left-handed melody) that fits the spirit of this music as the earnest solemnity of some of his younger colleagues would not.

Drummer Jo Jones needs no credentials, to be sure, but the appropriateness of his presence in this company might be pointed out. He brought a lightness and ease to jazz drumming rather like the lightness and ease which Carter brought to jazz playing and jazz writing. Here, he does *Cotton Tail,* for instance, with the responses of an intimate knowledge. Yet it isn't his piece, of course; it was originally

Ellington's and Ben Webster's with Sonny Greer on drums. Jones is decidedly a part of the exceptional swinging and creative groove that develops on Carter's blues *Doozy*. Jo Jones's fills between phrases are more spare than those of some of his younger colleagues perhaps, but the important thing is that they are never wrong.

Time and again Johnny Collins's guitar provides expert rhythmic and harmonic stability. But most outstanding is his ability to blend with the group: one is never aware of the sore-thumb *ching-a-ching* with which so much small-group rhythm guitar sticks out. Collins played with Carter's big band of the mid-forties and he has also worked with such illustrious jazzmen as Art Tatum, Roy Eldridge, Lester Young, and Dizzy Gillespie. Since 1951, he has worked with Nat "King" Cole.

Honeysuckle Rose begins and ends with Carter scoring based on the original version. Soloists in order are Rouse, Woods, Hawkins (entering from a very unexpected place), and Carter (notice his fine conclusion). Then four-bar phrases by each man in the same order.

The first slow piece is Quincy Jones's *The Midnight Sun Will Never Set:* Hawkins, Katz, and Carter contribute in that order.

Crazy Rhythm, the second memorial to the 1937 date, inspires, in 1961, a still exuberant Hawkins, then Woods, Rouse, a still-original Carter, and Katz.

Blue Star has the especially lovely, deceptively simple saxophone writing I have mentioned. Those variations the saxes play toward the end have been running through my own head since I first heard them, and that is about as high a tribute as I could pay them. The soloists are Hawkins on the theme-opening, with the decoratively improvised chorus by Carter. Katz has the bridge of the last chorus, with Carter ad-libbing a finish on the appropriately subdued ending.

On *Cotton Tail,* Carter has retained the nearly classic saxophone writing from the Ellington-Webster version. That's Hawkins who breaks through on the bridge of the first chorus. Then the order of sax solos is Carter, Rouse, Woods, and Hawkins.

The opening ensemble on *Body and Soul* is Carter's fresh and understanding scoring of Hawkins's still-classic 1939 version of the piece. Woods follows on the section writing, then Rouse, Carter, and Hawkins. Notice the bridge that Hawkins uses; it is based on an altered chord-sequence that Carter and Katz suggested in the studio. Hawkins chews up these new changes, and the coda he ad-libbed at the end had Charlie Rouse's jaw hanging open in amazed delight.

On *Cherry* Carter's opening leads into the sax section. Rouse takes the bridge in solo. The section swings together, bending the notes the way a good soloist does. Then we hear from Carter (use this one to demonstrate his real individuality and ease), Rouse (with some virtuoso runs), Woods, and Hawkins.

The soloists who contribute to the rocking groove on the blues *Doozy* are Katz (introducing at first), Woods (don't let anybody tell you he can't play the blues), Hawkins, Carter, Rouse, and then Katz in variation. Notice how Rouse at first returns to the melody to build his part—no doubt his three years with Thelonius Monk, who likes to use the theme in his solos, encouraged the practice.

Of course, one reason for the continuing reputation of men like Carter and Hawkins is that each is a professional and thoroughly dependable craftsman. Each is also more than that. We can discuss techniques easily, but a jazzman's artistry, after all, is not really arguable. It is a matter between him and every individual listener who hears him play. I can only say that I believe in the artistry of each man, and that my belief has been rewarded for a long time. (*1961*)

ટેૹ

CLASSIC TENORS
Coleman Hawkins and Lester Young

> (Contact CM-3—and more recently Doctor Jazz FW 38446—collected the Coleman Hawkins 1943 session that produced *The Man I Love,* an earlier Hawkins date with *How Deep Is the Ocean* and other selections, and the 1943 Lester Young titles *I Got Rhythm, I'm Fer It Too,* etc., with a group originally issued under Dickie Wells's name.) "As far as I'm concerned, I think Coleman Hawkins was the President first, right? When I first heard him I thought that was some great jazz I was listening to. As far as myself, I think I'm the second one. Not braggadocious, you know I don't talk like that."
>
> —Lester Young (to François Postif in 1959)

Many jazz LPs have good music to recommend them, but few have exceptional performances by great players. This LP has just that in the Coleman Hawkins version of *The Man I Love.* But it has more—inevitably in that it has more Hawkins from the same session, and in that it has Lester Young.

These recordings were originally made in 1943 for the Signature label, the rights to them have been passed around a bit since, and they were recently rescued as they were about to enter the maw of a New Jersey plastics plant. They are here presented by Contact Records in what seems to me excellent tape and LP transfer, and on clean and audible pressing surfaces.

Twenty years is a long time in jazz, and a long time can make some things sound dated. But there are only a few things here which sound dated.

The proprietor of Signature Records, Bob Thiele, was in the Coast Guard when these sessions were done, in the "military morale" department and stationed at Manhattan Beach. A fellow member of that outfit was a young drummer who was already making a name for himself among musicians, Shelly Manne. In those days, Thiele recorded for his own pleasure and not only picked his own leaders but sometimes the sidemen as well, according to his own taste.

He remembers the *Man I Love* session as happy and productive. He believes, but is not sure, that that piece was done in one take. He is sure that it was nearly destroyed when a clean-up man, carrying a wet mop, nearly walked in the studio in the middle of it. Thiele dashed out of the control room and blocked his way just in time.

The Dickie Wells-Lester Young session was originally done under Wells's name, and the personnel was obviously drawn from the Basie band of that period, except for Bill Coleman and Ellis Larkins. Larkins later became something of a mystery man, appearing often to play brilliantly, especially as an accompanist to singers, then disappearing. The Basie orchestra was doing a theatre date at the time, and the men were in the studio about midnight.

The first four selections in the Hawkins repertory were quite successful, especially among musicians. I can testify that anyone who entered a jazz nightclub in 1944 would probably hear *The Man I Love* performed at this interesting tempo and hear *Sweet Lorraine,* and probably *Get Happy* too, done in ways obviously inspired by these recorded performances. It was just about the hippest thing one could do just before everybody tried to emulate Parker and Gillespie a year or so later.

It was Hawkins's idea to do this rhythmic double-up on *The Man I Love.* After Manne's introduction, Heywood—then Eddie Heywood, Jr.—is the first soloist. Heywood Senior, by the way, did honorable service as a pianist and blues accompanist. And in the 1940s, Junior obviously was a jazz pianist (and not yet the author of such ditties as *Canadian Sunset*) with a style of his own that echoed Teddy Wilson and Nat "King" Cole. We also hear on this piece from Oscar Pettiford, then one of the most promising bassists in jazz (and a couple of years later, after he came to terms with bebop, one of the most fulfilled bassists in jazz).

Then, Hawkins. It is impossible truly to account for the excellence of Hawkins's solo on *The Man I Love* since it is impossible to explain musical excellence. But one can point out some of the things that contribute to it. There is Hawkins's tenor sound at this period, less hard and brittle than his sound in the thirties, and more appropriate, I think, to his manifestly expanding musical sophistication. The second is his rhythmic variety. At medium and fast tempos, Hawkins's phrasing usually sets up the expectation of a driving, regular accentuation: HEAVY beat, light beat/HEAVY, light/HEAVY, light/HEAVY, light/etc. The ingenuity comes when he breaks up that expectation with rhythmic surprises, as he does so well here. Then there is the variety in his melodic ideas here, as traditional-sounding riffs and blues phrases interplay with his more showy arpeggios—the latter being the technique of "playing out" the harmonies of a piece, playing the individual notes of a chord in succession (instead of all at once as they would be on a piano keyboard) to form melodies.

The Hawkins arpeggios are more predominant on *Sweet Lorraine* and he forms them into meaningful melodic phrases. This performance shows Hawkins's ballad style of the period. He does not use the more pronounced rhythmic manner of his faster tempos, but glides more easily from one heavy beat to the next, curving around the light beats. I am somewhat dismayed to remember how many fledgling pianists in the forties got credit for "originality" on *Sweet Lorraine* by alternating some of the ideas that Heywood plays here with other ideas that they borrowed from Nat "King" Cole's versions of the piece.

You might try this reading of *Get Happy* out on your novice friends: it shows how musicians transform the melody of a popular standard—the opening chorus here are close to the Harold Arlen original but are not exactly like it. Jazzmen do this in order to evolve themes that are closer to their own idiom, while retaining the harmonic challenge implicit in the original piece. Hawkins's final chorus is almost an anthology of the phrases players played (more often *were to play*) on this piece. Indeed, a couple of his fragments here were turned into "originals" by other musicians.

Crazy Rhythm was a second visit to the celebrated Hawkins vehicle of 1937, recorded in Paris with (among others) Benny Carter, Django Reinhardt. It also presents a Heywood solo of showy unobtrusiveness. (Hawkins and Carter recently did another *Crazy Rhythm,* by the way.)

> Dickie Wells [wrote André Hodeir in *Jazz: Its Evolution and Essence*] is majesty personified in style and particularly in tone. [Hodeir elaborated] "It seems incontestable that Wells is one of the most perfect constructors of choruses in

the history of jazz. He has not only a sense of contrast . . . but also . . . of balance. I mentioned . . . that he is a born romantic. I believe this is true in a certain sense, for few musicians have his vivid imagination, his sweeping ardor, his impetuous effervescence, and his profoundly dramatic accent; but these expressive qualities, which make him one of the most sensitive soloists, are supported by a firm foundation in his sense of balance, and this is what distinguishes him from equally admirable but less well organized musicians . . .

I can think of no other recordings which capture Dickie Wells's sound of this period better than these do. His entrance on *Linger Awhile* is so striking, I think, because of that sound: conveying humor yet with a hint of pain, with dignity yet with nothing of pompousness. Then there is his slow chorus on the blues *I'm Fer It Too* (introduced, please note, by a rare glimpse of guitarist Freddie Green in solo) with the burred edge and controlled vibrato of Wells's trombone, producing a sort of muted-horn without a mute—also achieved in part by humming into the horn as he plays.

"I developed my tenor to sound like an alto, to sound like a tenor, to sound like a bass . . ." said Lester Young in 1959. It was the "alto sound" that he began with and which at first brought him ridicule from some musicians. But Young did not give up the approach until he had explored it. Soon, having stuck to his convictions, Lester Young had not only reassessed the sound and aesthetic of his instrument, but had re-interpreted some of the basic grammar of jazz and had become one of the most influential players in the music.

The Lester Young we hear here is the one who was turning to the "tenor sound." These performances were made before his almost devastating fifteen months in the army which began in October 1944. He had just rejoined Basie at the time, having first left him in 1940.

The melody on *Hello Babe* is evidence of a growing sophistication: it is obviously a more developed line than the simpler riff-style pieces these men had been concocting a few years earlier.

One rule of thumb about Lester Young, the President, that this piece illustrates for me, is that he was a great player because you remember his musical ideas, you retain his melodic phrases.

This performance also offers the first taste of Bill Coleman in solo. He was a really excellent player in a style that fits right in with the Basie-ites. Coleman's work is much less well known that it should be because he has spent so much time as an expatriate, particularly in France, but with forays into India, Egypt, the Philippines, Japan, North Africa, and elsewhere.

Linger Awhile is an unexpected piece, but notice how Wells's solo immediately re-composes it as a jazz vehicle. It is Wells's voice incidentally, which calls out to Lester Young for his extra half-chorus before the quasi-Dixieland jam out. (How quaint is the slang of yesteryear! *Prez-arini!*)

I Got Rhythm of course has been number two in the jazz repertory, second only to the blues as a vehicle for improvising. Its outline had already provided Young with *Lester Leaps In,* and this version (which barely hints at Gershwin's original melody) presents him at a faster tempo, and in two, separated solos. I admit that I would complain that Larkins's "stride" brass under his second solo ties things down rhythmically in a somewhat less-than-ideal manner. Some of the great moments in recorded jazz for me come when Lester Young's solos take their marvelous free-handed approach to jazz rhythm, while Count Basie drops his left-hand stride and makes right-hand punctuations behind him. Lester

Young seems less than bothered by Larkins's regularity, however. And again, there is the intuitive order of his solo: he dances along with phrases of building complexity, and then airs everything out with a devastatingly simple idea or two. The unexpected always becomes logical with Lester Young, but only after he has shown us how it can be logical.

I'm Fer It Too is an unusual example of blues composing coming from these men. The solo-like theme is a continuous, two-chorus melody, broken in the second chorus by a four-bar piano solo. I have mentioned Wells's opening chorus, but I did not mention his later exchanges with Jo Jones. The tempo goes up when Lester Young enters, and one might be tempted to call this his "happy blues" mood except that Lester Young is far too complex a player for so simple a word as *happy*. It also seems to me that Bill Coleman's direct melodic statements come at just the right moment after Lester Young's intricate dance.

Perhaps the best way to end these notes is with a summary, but the best summary I could offer would be to repeat my opening sentence: Many jazz LPs have good music to recommend them, but few have exceptional performances by great players. *(1963)*

ॐ

ONCE THERE WAS BIRD
Charlie Parker

(The short-lived Parker label began with a collection of all the then-known takes from the very important 1945 Red Norvo Septet date with Charlie Parker and

Dizzy Gillespie. Soon after the LP appeared, by the
way, still another take of *Hallelujah* turned up and
saw issue in England. Indeed, after Parker Records col-
lapsed, Spotlite in England completed the Dial series.)

Most people who pick up a copy of this LP will have some
idea of who alto saxophonist Charlie Parker was and what
he contributed to jazz music. That is, most people will know
that Parker is supposed to have been one of the founders of
a music that was first called be-bop, and then modern jazz.
And the story is well known that the style evolved as certain
far-seeing players came together in experimental jam sessions in uptown New York in the early forties—at Minton's
Playhouse, with guitarist Charlie Christian until he died,
pianist Thelonious Monk, drummer Kenny Clarke, and
frequently trumpeter Dizzy Gillespie; or at Monroe's Uptown House, with alto saxophonist Charlie Parker and
again frequently trumpeter Dizzy Gillespie. Parker had a
falling-star career—his musical brilliance was acclaimed by
perceptive jazzmen; he was idolized and imitated; and he
was dead in March of 1955, of—among other things—frustration, personal indulgence, and probably self-recrimination
as well. Such are the facts of the matter as generally known.
Or perhaps only as generally assumed.
    One might reasonably maintain that anything recorded
by so brilliant an artist of such a short life as Charlie Parker
would be worth preserving. And one might argue, on the
other hand, that Parker should be remembered only by the
performances he selected himself for issue out of a given
recording date. But, as we shall see, things are not so simple.
There is more than one man involved in the record date,
and Parker may play his best on an early take of a tune
when the rest of the players have not quite got the piece
down. The best overall performance might be the one origi-

nally selected for 78 rpm release, but Parker himself may be better on an earlier take. And, as we shall also see, it is sometimes more than a little difficult to decide when a player of Parker's stature is best, because second- and even third-best may be brilliant.

One more or less technical note is in order. Not only have Charlie Parker's record dates (including those represented by this series) been issued in frequently chaotic disorder on LP, some have also appeared with grotesquely distorted sound. Dial made a strong and largely successful effort to be faithful to the sound of Charlie Parker's alto saxophone and to the overall character of his groups. And Dial was particularly successful on occasion in recording modern jazz drumming. We have tried to be just as faithful as possible to those achievements: we have added no spurious echo, no hyped-up highs and missing lows in faked "fidelity." And when there was a choice to be made between retaining a slight surface noise and rolling off the upper end of the music in order to get rid of it, we have always decided in favor of the music. This music was originally recorded before the days of tape, on acetate discs. In one or two of our alternate takes, these acetates themselves had a bit of scratch, and we will be frank to admit it in the notes. By and large we have decided in favor of musical considerations and of documentary completeness.

The session represented on this LP took place in June 1945 in New York. It was originally organized by vibraharpist Red Norvo, and was done for a label called Comet, which was later acquired by Dial. There were to be four numbers, intended for release on two 12-inch, 78 rpm records (which allowed for more playing time than the more usual 10-inch discs of the time). Besides Norvo, the personnel included another player firmly established in the thirties, Teddy Wilson, and two younger drummers both of whom have been fruitfully influenced by the flexibly great jazz drummer of that period (and perhaps all periods), Sidney Catlett. It included Flip Phillips, a younger soloist then with the highly successful Woody Herman band, whose roots actually lay in the thirties. The juxtaposition of Parker and Gillespie against these players, on a program of two up-tempo standards plus a slow and a medium blues, succinctly dramatizes both the innovative quality of their work and its firm and authentic heritage within the jazz tradition. Red Norvo, for example, has a trained and sophisticated concept of harmony and—listening to him here—one wonders if he could not take on just about any chord changes he wanted to. Yet Norvo sounds nothing like a modernist; in fact he sounds (although not in any bad sense) like the most old-fashioned player on the date. And obviously this is a matter of phrasing, of melodic rhythm, for it is Norvo's phrasing (which for him is entirely appropriate to the other elements of his style), the way he places his notes both against the basic rhythm and one after another, that makes him sound the way he does—quite aside from any questions of harmony, far out or far in. And it is the masterly freshness of their phrasing that immediately strikes one about Parker and Gillespie.

The date began (at a hellishly early morning hour, by the way) with *Hallelujah*. Wilson plays an intro, followed by Gillespie playing the theme, with the saxes in a little counter-motif behind him. Norvo enters fluently, and notice how deftly Specs Powell adapts his drumming to the vibist's style. Phillips's accents are very different. Unfortunately he seems the weakest soloist on this and several other pieces on the date. Wilson's glittering pianistic abilities should not obscure the musical ideas he gets going here, particularly in the bridge and after. Gillespie follows the pianist in the starkest contrast, really tearing through. But it is not mere bravura display, for one idea after another comes from his horn, and he certainly does not seem to need the support of that Woody Herman-ish (or rather "First Herd"-ish) sax riff behind him. Slam Stewart's bass solo, like all his solos, is bowed and hummed at the same time. But such gimmickry is only the surface; he sets up a constantly fanciful and varied continuity of riff figures, with great good humor. Parker's solo is almost a warmup in that he seems to repeat one idea several times. As we shall see, Parker could use such an approach to organize his solos quite brilliantly but here the effect is repetitious. The final chorus here sounds to me like a Gillespie variation. At any rate, it was typical of the time in that it is in the new idiom, but has some of the old phrasing and brevity of phrase clinging to it. (Modernist pieces like *Shaw 'Nuff, Billie's Bounce,* and *Anthropology* break away completely.)

The second take of *Hallelujah* is faster and surer. Notice Wilson's accompaniment to Norvo's two choruses—almost modern comping. In solo, Wilson here is more scalar and less melodic than before. Gillespie is even more assertive. Parker, again taking off under Stewart's final notes, simply takes over. He was ready this time, fully, and he plays a commanding chorus. Then Parker and Gillespie play the final ensemble variation together, in one of those moments of breathtaking unity that they could bring off, but which got recorded all too infrequently. This, like all the final takes on this LP, was the one originally issued by Comet.

You will notice that our two takes of *Get Happy* begin with number 3; the first two were apparently very fragmentary or otherwise uninteresting and never appeared. Wilson takes the bridge of the first chorus, and each subsequent solo begins with a "break," a suspension of the rhythm. Norvo really goes after the chord changes. Gillespie here is somewhat calmer than on the previous piece. And we hear a rare Charlie Parker, the "cool" Parker of the celebrated *Yardbird Suite*. It is also like the very early Parker to be heard on the 1941-42 Jay McShann records. This is surely one of the most valuable of all Parker alternate takes. And the chorus contains a hint of the brilliant way he could organize a solo with echo phrases that are not repetitive, as he begins the last eight bars of his chorus with an elaboration of a previous phrase. Wilson is fluently effective behind the final chorus, and that chorus again sounds like a Gillespie variation—but of course we may never know who actually originated this counter theme to *Get Happy*. This take dissolves into talk after the final bridge.

On the second *Get Happy*, the rhythm seems to rush a bit under Phillips; he was apparently having trouble with ideas and perhaps there was an effort to bolster him. Gillespie holds exuberance and musical ideas in a tantalizing balance. His solo, by the way, contains phrases which were imitated to death during the next few years by almost a whole generation of young trumpeters. Here Parker approaches the piece quite differently but comes up with an equally sustained chorus, except perhaps for his last eight bars.

On the second side of the LP we have the various takes of two blues, with a new drummer, J. C. Heard, invited in from a nearby studio at Gillespie's suggestion. *Slam Slam Blues* is of course for Stewart, who announces again, after Wilson's melodic introduction, that it would be impossible for him not to be genuinely humorous, even at this slow tempo and in this blues mood. Then Parker: perhaps the most authentic slow blues player on the date, yet the most personal and original. Parker could "play the blues," even as Gillespie in this sense cannot. Wilson offers very good melodic phrases, and Gillespie seems unusually pensive. This I think is Phillips's best solo—and his most Ben Webster-ish, it seems to me. The shouting Dixie-like ending is on both takes (and incidentally this first take was once issued with the title *Bird Blues*). On the second take, Parker opens with essentially the same phrase, and then proceeds to organize a rather different kind of chorus. On the former he alternated simple lines with complex lines—something like his famous *Parker's Mood* solo. Here he builds gradually from simplicity to complexity. Again Gillespie is lyric, here almost ballad-like.

   Congo Blues is represented by two fragments and three takes; the fragments each preserve two Gillespie choruses. Notice that on the first, he plays one muted chorus and then one on open horn, but subsequently uses the mute on both. (That drum intro perhaps has a little bit more to do with Brazil than the Congo, by the way.) It is Parker who breaks off both of these fragments (although that may be Gillespie calling to him on the first one). The confusion perhaps comes from the fact that the *Congo Blues* solos are supposed to open with four bars of stop-time followed by a full twelve-bar solo. The surface noise audible in the second fragment was present in the original acetate, but it preserves a full chorus of Parker after Gillespie's two. By the third take, J. C. Heard's intro is even surer and the trumpeter plays with wonderful fluency. But the altoist is still slightly imperfect. The fourth take (this is its first LP appearance by the way) finds Parker executing much more surely and coming up with more complex ideas. Wilson's phrasing has a charming looseness on this one, and Stewart is firmly assertive. The closing riff here is different from the one used on the other takes, but both of them are slight variants of stock riffs from the early modern repertory, to be sure. The final *Congo Blues* was perhaps the best choice for original release. Gillespie plays with amazing rapidity and fluency, but again, the technique is handmaiden to musical ideas. Parker plays the sort of chorus we alluded to above; it is brilliantly cohesive because key melodic phrases are echoed parallel and fragmented as his melody unfolds.

This session marked only the ninth time that Charlie Parker had ever entered a studio for a commercial record date. On three of those nine he was a sideman with the Jay McShann orchestra, and on two, he was one of several players accompanying vocalists. On this date he was, for the fourth time, a sideman in an instrumental group. Yet he was already a major contributor to an important movement in American music. Perhaps *the* important contributor. And the movement is by now one of the glories in the mainstream of jazz. (*1962*)

ट‍➷

MILES DAVIS
Walkin'

(The Miles Davis *"Walkin'"* date was originally issued on 12-inch LP as Prestige 7076. The issue for which these notes were written was Prestige 7608. The selections discussed were of course subsequently collected in the twelve-disc set of Davis's complete 1951-56 Prestige recordings.)

Walkin' and *Blue 'n' Boogie,* a classic session. What to say about it? That it carries its years (It was recorded April 29, 1954) superbly? That music largely made up on the spur of the moment that long ago was exceptionally meaningful then, and still is now? Yes. But surely there is more to say about a classic session, a recorded jam session that is also a work of art.

It came at an important moment for jazz of the era. The "modern jazz," founded by Dizzy Gillespie, Charlie Parker and their associates was then a little over ten years old. The participants gathered for what pianist Dick Katz has called "an amazing seminar." For in these excellent performances, so immediately effective even at a casual listening, there is also going on a reassessment of the materials, the devices, and the aims of jazz. As Katz put it, "a sort of summing up of much of what happened musically to the players involved during the preceding ten years . . . It's as if all agreed to get together to discuss on their instruments what they had learned and unlearned, what elements of bop they had retained or discarded."* And how absolutely right it was that such a high-level musical discourse should have taken place on the blues!

Davis, of course, had been an associate of Charlie Parker since the saxophonist's first date as a leader. And, somewhat influenced no doubt by a trumpeter named Freddy Webster, Davis had brought a very different sensibility to the music than Gillespie or the directly Gillespie-influenced trumpeters like Fats Navarro and Howard McGhee had offered. When the idiom first found itself an authentic trombonist, it was J. J. Johnson, and he had been associated with Parker on records by 1947. Lucky Thompson's roots obviously lie more directly in the styles of the previous era, but he is in several respects a modernist in the mid-1940s' sense, and he had recorded as a Dizzy Gillespie and a Charlie Parker sideman by 1946. Horace Silver was a comparative newcomer when these dates were done, but an obviously impor-

* From *Jazz Panorama*.

tant one, who played, one might put it, like a cross between Bud Powell and a first-rate barroom bluesman. Percy Heath has said that he undertook music when he was captivated by a Charlie Parker record he heard on the radio. Kenny Clarke, a man beyond category to be sure, virtually founded "modern" jazz drumming.

Walkin' is an exceptionally strong, and well-named, blues theme, a combination of modern and traditional-sounding ideas that, incidentally, involves a discreet use of the flatted fifths which second-rate boppers had made into a cliché. And the unison rendition of the theme by trumpet-trombone-tenor sounds so good not only because of the instruments but also because of the trumpet, trombone, and tenor players involved, and the way they understand each other's sounds.

Davis's solo is a model of clarity, sound ideas, logic, and sustained feeling. Johnson's solo has the same clarity and ease, and is virtually a summary of his accomplishments.

Lucky Thompson, whose rhythmic idiom was more traditional, builds up his solo rather differently, more overtly and dramatically than Davis and Johnson—the contrast between his approach and theirs is also just right for the overall effect of the performance—and he is effectively helped as Davis and Johnson enter behind him with an abstraction of the theme at precisely the right moment.

Horace Silver's two choruses state the particular kind of funky modern piano he played at the time. But do not miss Silver throughout, for the background of sympathetic feeling and structural ideas he provides each hornman is rare. Heath plays as usual with the love of his instrument and love of the music and his fellow musicians that is his own. And Kenny Clarke performs on the level of the hornmen, understanding and animating each player. He and Silver also work beautifully together: where Silver is percussive, Clarke is smooth, yet there is never a negative or distractingly personal tension set up between them.

Blue 'n' Boogie proceeds along in the same kind of theme-and-solos plan. Dizzy Gillespie's theme, his striking 1945 reassessment of some traditional ideas, is here played with the kind of controlled intensity that has characterized the best jazz since King Oliver. Davis is more extraverted here, and, somewhat surprisingly at this faster tempo, his agile solo is occasionally more elaborate. At the same time, his phrases are aired out with the frugal use of space and rest of which he is a master. Again, Johnson avoids clichés. And notice the figures from Davis and Johnson that aid Thompson's climactic chorus this time.

The same superb rhythm section appears on the second side of this LP, on a session which took place earlier the same month, on April 3, 1954, with Davis and Davey Schildkraut as the horns. Schildkraut was called "an ornithologist" by Ira Gitler in his original notes to this LP, in acknowledgment of his debt to Charlie Parker. He is also a cool ornithologist. At this point, his pure and somewhat lonely sound had been heard with the like of Stan Kenton and Pete Rugolo.

The session is a rare and relatively early statement of how Davis had made a combination of trumpet sound, mute, and a highly creative use of the microphone into one of the most personal and effective musical sonorities in jazz history. And the theme *Solar* is perhaps an ideal opening vehicle for that sound.

Solar, which might be called a trip halfway to the moon (or perhaps half a degree in ornithology),* has the kind of melody that is fresh when one first hears it, and also mem-

---

* That is, it uses sixteen measures of the chords to *How High the Moon;* *Ornithology* uses the full thirty-two.

orable—partly because of the way Davis states it of course; it is the kind of theme that, once one has heard, he catches himself whistling unconsciously, and often. *Solar*'s chord changes, its harmonic under-structure, alluded to above, was a favorite in the earliest days of Parker and Gillespie, and thus this performance also features the kind of reassessment and reevaluation heard on the other side of this LP.

You Don't Know What Love Is is one of those exceptional examples of intense ballad interpretations (intense, but also melancholy and almost wistful) that tell us something essential about Miles Davis's musical character, and that sometimes evoke comparisons of Davis to Louis Armstrong. (I am not sure that Davis entirely appreciates the comparisons, but I do know of his generous tribute to the older trumpeter: "You know, you can't play anything on a horn that Louis hasn't played—I mean even modern. I love his approach to the trumpet; he never sounds bad . . .")

Love Me or Leave Me is taken fast, and for me, the honors go to Horace Silver's energetic, allusive, sometimes comic, eventful solos, particularly his first, done in conversation with the horns. In the second, he typically gets in a reminder of *My Man*. And watch that rumbling, barking left hand.

Miles Davis's comments on Louis Armstrong, quoted above, were evoked by Armstrong's 1927 recording of *Potato Head Blues,* and were made over thirty years later. It would be easy to imagine, thirty years from now, a young jazz trumpeter paying tribute to both Armstrong and Davis. For Davis, his remarks might easily be inspired by *Walkin'.* (*1968*)

ॐ

MILES DAVIS AND THE MODERN JAZZ GIANTS

(As indicated below, the Miles Davis–Milt Jackson–
Thelonious Monk *The Man I Love* date, as it has
come to be called, first appeared on several Prestige
LPs before the issue discussed below—Prestige 7650—
brought all its music together. I have here added to
those original notes some comments on Milt Jackson
borrowed from my notes to Prestige 7655 *"The Complete Milt Jackson and Horace Silver."* Subsequently,
the music discussed below was also included in the
Prestige two-LP set *"Tallest Trees"* (P-24012) and of
course in the boxed *"Complete Miles Davis."*)

The *Bags' Groove—Man I Love* date, all of it, collected on
a single LP. Miles Davis, Milt Jackson, Thelonious Monk,
Percy Heath, and Kenny Clarke, Christmas eve, 1954. That,
to the initiate, is perhaps all that needs to be said.

It is all here: the often fascinating "second" takes; the
mistakes (even on some of the "first" takes); the evidence
of the bickering disagreements that went on in the studio;
and the glories—some of the most brilliant "modern" jazz
that ever got recorded, and including moments of genius.

Bags' Groove is of course Milt Jackson's pentatonic blues
theme, a very special one which manages to sound earthy,
traditional, and modern all at once. On "take 1," Davis and
Jackson, with a bit of part juggling, state that theme beautifully. Davis's solo—clean, economical, apparently gentle and
vocal, but still forceful—is, like much of his best improvising, a memorable chain of linking ideas.

Davis is accompanied only by Heath and Clarke. Each is

an exceptional player, of course, but the excellence with which they work together here is also a result of the time they had spent together in the Modern Jazz Quartet.

The contrast of Milt Jackson's entrance with Monk suddenly behind him is superb, in timing, sonority, and style. Jackson sounds somewhat more conservative here than the other soloists. And Monk accompanies, not with blues changes, but—like an improvising composer-orchestrator of a rare sort—with textures, rhythmic contrasts and complements, a virtual counterpoint of interesting but never interfering ideas.

Monk's own solo, deceptively simple on the surface perhaps, is one of the great moments of recorded jazz. Pianist Dick Katz has written in *Jazz Panorama* that "By an ingenious use of space and rhythm, and by carefully controlling a single melodic idea, he builds a tension that is not released until the end of his solo. . . . His sense of structure and his use of extension is very rare indeed. And it *sounds good*." André Hodeir speaks, in *Toward Jazz*, of the "tremendous pressure" which Monk, in his disjunct phrasing and pregnant silences, exerts on his listeners. And Hodeir even singles out the detail of the "shattering" effect in Monk's first chorus of the F sharp that follows the series of C's and F's "one of the purest moments of beauty in the history of jazz."

And the solo as a whole is one of the most prophetic I would add. It does not so much link ideas, one to the next, as Davis did, as it airily spins out of itself, out of its own opening phrase—as both Katz and Hodeir indicate. And, although one could readily tick off the number of blues choruses involved, the solo virtually floats above its chord changes and their implied four-bar phrases, determining its own character as it goes along. Indeed, in 1954, Monk outlined the major tasks of the new jazz of the 1960s.

Bags' Groove "take 2" has a less cleanly played "head," and the contrast can teach a layman something about ensemble playing. Davis seems to be having some saliva problems with his horn but still lifts the performance and keeps his lines swingingly alive. Jackson is as good here as on the other take, I believe. Monk in his solo is, for him, more conventional.

Bemsha Swing was evidently done earlier in the date when Monk was still accompanying Davis, before Davis, who would rather have supportive chord changes behind him, had asked him to lay out during this solo. What does happen is that they get into a kind of musical argument: at one point Davis plays a favorite Monk lick, Monk responds, and for a while they have it out, back and forth.

Jackson plays on his best level. And Monk's solo, as Dick Katz has put it, "Is a fine example of his ability to construct variations on a theme (in this case his own), rather than discard it and build 'lines' on the chords . . ." Monk uses two approaches here: he embellishes and fills out his theme; then he simplifies and abstracts it.

"Take 1" of *The Man I Love* begins with a fine Jackson introduction, falls into verbal disagreements, with Davis's finishing it off with his request to engineer Rudy Van Gelder (herewith fulfilled) to "put this on a record, all of it." Then there is an even better Jackson intro, and the performance begins. Either of Miles Davis's glowing abstractions of this theme might stand with his best and most personal melodic paraphrases, which means with some of the best in jazz history. I do admit, however, that I prefer the second. Jackson takes a break and doubles the tempo and swirls through the changes for two choruses. Monk, his humor with him as always, and his percussive originality much to the fore, undertakes to spread out the main strain of the piece in long meter, get in tempo for the bridge, then stretch it out again for the last eight bars. It works on the first eight bars (and there is nothing quite like this performance until Monk's first solo version of *I Should Care*). It doesn't work on the second; he stops; Heath and Clarke walk gracefully; and Miles calls Monk back into the bridge. Each performance ends with Davis evoking the original ballad tempo and mood, and the others briefly joining him for the ravishingly abstract conclusion.

Milt Jackson is a paradox of spirit and sensitivity. The spirit was there. You can hear it in his earliest records. The sensitivity developed. But it developed so naturally, and related itself so perfectly to the spirit, that hearing him one assumes it was all there from the beginning.

In *Toward Jazz,* Hodeir went so far as to say that his early work might deceive us in what it promised. "When he began playing the vibraphone, his style was rather dry, metallic, and aggressive, deliberately lacking in charm; today his instrument has a limpid, ethereal, and at times almost disembodied sound, as though he had the power to make us forget the impact of the mallet on the bars, to absorb it completely. . . . His style has gained in self-assurance, his phrasing has become suppler and better ventilated; in a slow tempo he will make very free use of different rhythmic values . . . Moreover, Bags has managed to resolve the conflict between excessive harshness and excessive sentimentality that once hampered his style . . ."

The vibraharp—think about it—is a strange instrument. Classed as a percussive because it is struck rather than blown or stroked or bowed, it might be called a metallic xylophone. To make matters apparently worse, the basis for some of its subtleties of sound is a series of small mechanically operated, electrically run fans that move the air and affect the tones produced by the mallet on the keys. Yet jazzmen have raised the vibes to the level of a most expressive melody instrument. And none have raised it higher than Milt Jackson, for he is not only a great player, but a great soloist—and remember that it is possible to be the former in jazz without being the latter.

Swing Spring is Davis's little scaler piece, inspired, he has said, by Bud Powell. (It also echoes the "cool" Davis of 1948-50.) "You play in that scale and you get an altogether different sound," he once remarked of *Swing Spring*. Here he demonstrates it and, once again, we are into the tasks that jazz took up again in the 1960s. Jackson plays in his best straight-ahead, medium-tempo style, with Monk in occasionally brilliant rhythmic contrast behind him. Miles returns (with some minor technical problems) and in his last chorus ends up calling to Monk with (again) one of the pianist's favorite phrases. More by-play! Monk himself uses a variant of the phrase. Then he airily tries out, in new ways, some of the ideas which, on other occasions, the *I Got Rhythm* chord changes have suggested to him. Jackson takes a second solo, and at a couple of spots Monk is typically witty behind him.

As I say, some mistakes, some bickering (verbal and musical), choruses of excellence and of brilliance, and moments of genius.

Rare qualities, those last.   (*1969*)

🦆

THELONIOUS MONK
The Golden Monk

> (The two quintet sessions represented on *"The Golden Monk"* on Prestige 7053 and later 7363 had previously appeared simply as *"Monk"* on Prestige, and have since reappeared on Original Jazz Classics OJC-010. The music of this and the following record has also appeared in the Prestige two-disc album P-24006.)

The mid-1960s find Thelonious Monk a famous man—almost a celebrity. But it did not take him until the mid-1960s to develop into a major jazz musician. Monk had been that for almost twenty years before fame caught up with him.

Take the LP recording at hand: it contains a great deal of good Monk, some exceptional Monk, and, in his transformation of *Smoke Gets in Your Eyes,* one of the best things he has ever done. Yet these recordings were made at possibly the lowest point of his career. He could not work in New York City because he did not have the necessary permit, the so-called "cabaret card." But one wonders, even if Monk had had a card, what club-owners would have employed him in 1953 and 1954.

Many people had heard about Monk before they had ever heard his music. He was always credited by early modern jazzmen with having been a major participant in the Minton's jam sessions that helped develop the music. Monk's earliest records (he started recording in 1947) may have satisfied some people's curiosities, but at the time they left many others puzzled and dismayed about exactly what he was doing. It was not until 1958 that musicians and insiders really began to rediscover Monk as a major composer and musician, and to recognize that he had seemed puzzling only because he was a thoroughly personal and original jazzman.

In all the years of his neglect, however, Monk stuck to his convictions about his music. And in the music on this record you will hear no evidence, in style or musical emotion, of the then-low state of his career.

Monk's music has been called difficult and obscure. And Monk's piano playing has been called simple. On the face of it, those two strictures might seem to cancel each other out, but, oddly, they frequently came from the same source. I confess the first one makes no sense at all to me; I can see nothing difficult in the quite straightforwardly melodious Monk compositions on this LP, although I can see a great deal that is commendably subtle in them. Actually, some of Monk's best pieces are built on traditional jazz phrases and ideas, which he handles and develops in a strikingly individual way. And I can see nothing difficult in the equally melodious Monk solos, some of which are as obviously based on the melodies themselves—try the first take of *Think of One,* or try *Locomotive,* or try *Hackensack.*

I can see why some commentators have called Monk a "simple" pianist, but I can't agree with them. From the obvious point of view of manual technique, notice on *Smoke Gets in Your Eyes,* how the outside fingers of Monk's right hand carry the melody while the inside fingers and thumb of the same hand make decorative trills. Or listen on *We See* to the original technique Monk has developed for bending an unbendable piano note. (He does it by a special manipulation of finger pressures and positions, and foot pedal.) However, on a less obvious level, Monk is a virtuoso player in terms of jazz and the jazz tradition: he is a master

of rhythm, time, accent; a man for whom delay, space, open-
ness, fleeting silence, and the unexpected accent are primary
aspects of musical expression.

Let's Call This is the first of three titles here that seem to
derive from the fact that when asked, Monk apparently
had no title. (But, he would "think of one" or he answered,
"We'll see.") *Let's Call This* is a strong melody—personally,
I have vividly remembered it since the first time I heard it—
and the combination of Julius Watkins's French horn,
Sonny Rollins's tenor saxophone, and Monk's piano, display
it with intriguing sound. It has a vocal quality, yet, like
Monk's best themes, it is not really a "song," since it was
obviously conceived to be played on instruments and
couldn't be sung to its best advantage. Its feeling of suspense
comes about because, technically, Monk does not resolve
things until the very end. And its feeling of continuity
comes about partly because the bridge, the release, the middle part of *Let's Call This* is a development of the main
melody—a typical Monkian touch. Rollins is inventive, but
his ideas never stray beyond the implications or mood of
Monk's theme. The saxophonist has always had a rapport
with Monk's presence and an understanding of Monk's music—Monk's phrasing, Monk's melodies, his harmonies, his
rhythm. In his solo, Monk is also inventive; he does not use
his *Let's Call This* melody itself but his graceful solo lines
are similarly appropriate.*

On *Think of One*, the second take, Monk again invents
fresh melodies in his solo. The piece has a challenge Monk
likes and has used elsewhere. It is built around one note.
Rhythmically, Rollins's solo takes a personal approach, in
an appropriate contrast to Monk both as composer and

---

* I should add that I had known *Let's Call This* for years before I heard
that its chords derive from the venerable *Sweet Sue*, so originally had
Monk handled them.

player. And listen to the pianist's chording behind Julius Watkins's French horn—even in fairly conventional piano "comping" (something he rarely offers), Monk is a subliminal melodist. Then, there is Monk's second solo, a spare, intriguing, tissue of notes, an example of how he uses musical space and of how tellingly he can distill and abstract a theme.

I value the first take of *Think of One* too. Monk's introduction is a succinct example of his quick musical wit, and this time both his solos find him using his theme. We can hear Rollins and Watkins learning, soaking up the music—and note how much Watkins particularly has learned from one take to the next of *Think of One*.

The other side of the LP offers Monk with Art Blakey—one of the most fruitful musical relationships in all of jazz. We hear one of Monk's favorite trumpeters, Ray Copeland. And Frank Foster, for years Count Basie's soloist and composer, is a man with a straight-ahead tenor style that helps enhance both the traditional and the original aspects of Monk's music.

We See is another Monk line which sings at the same time that it is clearly instrumental. Monk's own solo here is fluent, almost bristling, but his bridge is contrastingly simple and finds him twirling and catching one of his favorite phrases.

Locomotive is an aptly titled piece, and an exceptional example of how simple ideas do not sound obvious when Monk takes hold of them. He uses two brief, repeated figures, both played with fine momentum, setting one (on Copeland's trumpet) against the other (on Foster's sax). Copeland's dancing lyric phrases show, I think, why Monk favors the trumpeter so much. Notice how Monk train-whistles the theme back in during his brief closing solo.

Hackensack is built on a "standard" chord sequence.* (If the blues is sequence number one, and *I Got Rhythm* is number two, then one might call these nice girl changes number three.) The basic idea, the opening phrase of the melody here, has been around for a long time. *Hackensack* gives Monk's particular development of that idea, but it's quite possible the whole thing was his in the first place. There are several jazz "originals" from the early modern days that were not credited to Monk but are actually his.

I have saved Monk's superb transmutation of *Smoke Gets in Your Eyes* for final comment, although it is programmed earlier.

One might call *Smoke Gets in Your Eyes* a miniature concerto; the soloist leads the group but both share the total effect. It is a superb example of the Monkian alchemy by which a song is transformed into a composition for instruments. Monk's musical ideas, his splitting up of the theme, his appropriate piano embellishments, his deeply forceful playing, his commitment only to the best aspects of the piece—these things rid it of its sentimentality and of its prettiness, and leave it with only its implicit beauty and strength. (*1964*)

* *Oh, Lady Be Good.*

THELONIOUS MONK
The High Priest

("*The High Priest*"—Prestige 7508—had been the Monk trios on Prestige 7027 and later 7159, titled simply "*Thelonious Monk*." That version was reproduced as an Original Jazz Classic on OJC-016, and the music is included in the Prestige two-LP P-24006.)

It all starts here, with Thelonious Monk at the piano.

Monk has recorded with large jazz ensembles of at least two different kinds, and with small ensembles of from four through seven pieces. He is a major jazz composer and a unique performer.

But the music starts here with Monk on piano, working alone on one selection, or with bass and drums on the others, improvising on his own pieces and on standards. If the music isn't here with Monk on piano, it won't be there for a quartet or a septet or an orchestra. The music is here.

Pianist Bill Evans has written that Thelonious Monk is "an exceptionally uncorrupted creative talent." Largely uninfluenced by any musical tradition except that of American popular music and jazz, he has replaced formal superficialities with "fundamental structure" and produced "a unique and astoundingly pure music."

"Make no mistake," Evans continued. "This man knows exactly what he is doing in a theoretical way . . . We can be further grateful to him for combining aptitude, insight, drive, compassion, fantasy, and whatever else makes the 'total' artist . . . in an age of insurmountable conformist pressures."

In the past, Monk has been spoken of and written of as a sort of "musicians' musician," whose work was largely inaccessible to the public. First he was a somewhat obscure figure who had influenced the early be-boppers, including Dizzy Gillespie and Bud Powell. In the mid-fifties, he was known as an influence on saxophonists like Sonny Rollins and, later, John Coltrane. Now, of course, Monk is no longer written of as inaccessible. He has become very much the public's musician. But in retrospect, these trio recordings may make one wonder why he wasn't the public's musician all along.

In 1961 Monk named this version of *Blue Monk*, recorded in 1954, as a personal favorite among his own recordings, and he may very well still feel that way about it. It was a revelation to many listeners when it was first issued. Here was Monk, the supposedly eccentric almost legendary, "far out" pianist-composer, playing blues as fundamental as Jimmy Yancey's, as witty as Count Basie's (witty in a very different way to be sure), but still as personal as seemed possible. Monk the modernist was revealed as basically a blues man in the great tradition.

The performance is exceptional: spontaneous and with a wonderful momentum, but still with a fine inevitability about it. The interplay between Blakey and Monk is of a high order and beautifully affirms what several other tracks here indicate: that Blakey is *the* drummer for Monk. And *Blue Monk* is revealed as fundamental Monk: idea after idea, phrase after phrase, echo his other pieces and his other performances, yet everything fits in here as integral and necessary to *Blue Monk*.

There are three examples here of Monk's approach to popular songs: the solo version of *Just a Gigolo*, melancholy almost to the point of tragedy, and the trio version of *Sweet and Lovely*, a piece which this Monk performance re-intro-

duced into the jazz repertory, and *These Foolish Things.*
Now popular songs are written to be sung, and sung even
by the likes of you and me, with our probably small voices.
Monk's piano sings out these pieces (hear *Sweet and Lovely*
for a start), but at the same time Monk is not merely playing these songs on a piano and incidentally decorating them.
He gets inside them and remakes them into piano pieces.

Take *These Foolish Things.* Monk's intro may remind
you of the song *Please, Mr. Sun,* but notice the way it also
reshuffles the opening phrase of *These Foolish Things* itself.
From then on, Monk takes the piece in long-meter—to put
that differently, the beat is doubled-up on what it would
ordinarily be when the melody is taken this way. The piece
is also re-phrased. It is clashingly and sardonically underlined with minor seconds. And whatever additions Monk
makes to it are not simply decorations hung onto the melody but intrinsic parts of the performance. (For the novice,
by the way, singing along with the record, using a more conventional version of the piece will probably bring out all
these fine qualities.)

Monk the pianist and performer approaches his own ballads very much the same way. *Reflections* and particularly
Monk's Dream are the sort of striking, song-like pieces that
seem to cry out, when one first hears them, for a lyricist,
but that is not because they lack something as piano performances here.

Bemsha Swing was written in the 1940s in collaboration
with drummer Denzil Best. It might be called youthful
Monk therefore, but it went unrecorded until this 1952 version. Notice how Monk tosses isolated fragmentations of his
main theme at Max Roach during the latter's drum solo—"a
fascinating touch," Gunther Schuller once called it.

Little Rootie Tootie is Monk's train piece, punctuated
by tone-clustered whistle effects, and therefore distant rela-

tive to the train pieces that most blues pianists used to feature. I remember seeing a group of musicians, hearing this recording while rehearsing Hall Overton's big band arrangement of *Little Rootie Tootie*. They expressed spontaneous delight with the descending figure, and its wonderfully abrupt, witty conclusion, that moves Monk into the bridge of the third (final) chorus here.

Bye-Ya is Monk's "Latin" piece which has been picked up by several other musicians and lately been re-cast as a bossa nova. Notice how Monk has built his bridge out of the most traditional of phrases, but without merely repeating a cliché. The same sort of thing happens on the shimmering *Trinkle Tinkle* (an aptly named and truly a *pianistic* composition), where Monk has employed a florid figure often used by some of the old-time boogie woogie blues men as the basis of his theme.

Thelonius Monk has often been called "inimitable," and for him the word seems completely justified. Anyone can learn from him, anyone from pianists through hornmen, and as I've indicated above, many have. But so personal is his style that anyone who tries to *imitate* this unique musician directly will probably sound absurd. Monk himself, however, sounds anything but absurd. He is all music. And clearly the music begins here, with Monk at the piano. (*1967*)

ह&

SONNY ROLLINS
Saxophone Colossus

(Prestige 7326 was a repackaging of the earlier album of the same name and catalogue number by Rollins, Tommy Flanagan, Doug Watkins, and Max Roach. Prestige P-24050, a two-LP set, added selections from a Rollins-Clifford Brown date of the same period. The single *"Colossus"* LP is still available as these words are written however.)

To go directly to the point, this is one of the classic LPs of modern jazz. It captures a great player in the discovery of greatness. It offers much exceptional music. And in *Blue 7* it contains one of the truly successful extended performances on records.

I think you sense the importance of this music immediately, as you sense the sureness and the authority of almost every phase that Sonny Rollins plays here. You hear the combination of power and ease in his horn, and you know that the promising young tenor player has become a masterful jazz musician.

But there is more to it than that. Besides the emotional impact, there is an acute musical intelligence at work here and the performances represent a rare combination of spontaneous feeling and musical thoughtfulness, of emotional immediacy and affirmative order.

Inevitably the growing musical maturity of the Sonny Rollins of mid-1956 is not without its basis in the facts of Sonny Rollins's personal life. This LP was made when Rollins was a member of the Clifford Brown-Max Roach quintet. He had joined the group a few months earlier in Chicago at the climax of a period of rigorous self-assessment and personal and musical discipline, reflection, and study.

For me, each track this session illustrates a particular quality of Rollins's complex expressiveness as a player—although that being said I also realize that each track inevitably has many other of his good qualities as well.

St. Thomas, for example. It is Rollins's version of a traditional Caribbean calypso, chosen in tribute to the saxophonist's West Indian heritage. The performance might stand as a definitive example of Rollins's impeccable swing. That quality is especially notable after the first chorus, as Rollins juxtaposes his own North American jazz phrasing against Max Roach's continuing modified-Latin accompaniment. And Rollins's sense of order also emerges. Notice how he builds his first solo around his opening idea, the phrase he states immediately after he has ended the melody. Then, the performance gets an effective climax as everyone shifts into jazz rhythm after Roach's choruses. And Tommy Flanagan's piano solo is one of several examples here of how his gentle, shining virtuosity is in effective contrast to the stronger statements of Rollins and Roach.

I might pick *You Don't Know What Love Is* as an example of how Rollins can use dynamics, from the boldest of tenor cries to the softest whispered notes, and how he commands a full rich sound over the entire range of his horn (all this, by the way, in contrast to some of his imitators who say everything in a shout at middle range). And we hear Rollins's pervasive humor, sometimes sardonic to be sure, but never either ridiculing his material or pumping his ego. All of these qualities—his dynamics, his range and his tasteful humor—are parts of an integrated, original, and thoroughly unsentimental approach to ballads, as is also Rollins's firm, vibrato-less, almost cello-like tenor saxophone sound. We

open, of course, with a theme-statement of the piece, delivered with Rollins embellishments. Again, there is his or-
derliness, as the second chorus interplays original but appropriate melodies with occasional echoes and fragments of the
piece, which gradually disappear. There is an effective
chorus in double-time. Admittedly, far too many musicians
double-time their ballads as a cover-up because they can't
sustain a ballad mood or can't swing at a slower tempo.
Clearly Rollins can do both those things, and his double-
time episode is a legitimate part of a sustained design, a different sort of rhythmic exploration of the piece.

The title *Strode Rode* is for the Strode Lounge in Chicago, the place where Rollins first reentered music during
his year of self-examination and study. Notice how perfectly Rollins and Roach pronounce the staccato notes in
the theme together. The first chorus offers a new texture
from the group with Rollins and Doug Watkins working in
duo. Roach hints at his own reentry before he rolls himself
and Tommy Flanagan fully back into the piece in one of its
effective moments. Roach's responsiveness to Rollins's melodic ideas is excellent here, but things work the other way
too, and the conversation in four-bar phrases between Rollins and Roach on this piece is something of a minor marvel.
Sometimes Rollins delivers an almost percussive fragment
on his horn, sometimes a highly melodic phrase; Roach
responds with drum patterns, some of which almost sing
with melody.

But if I were to pick the single quality that *Strode Rode*
best illustrates for me it is the discipline with which Sonny
Rollins can use his saxophone technique, holding back his
most complex phrases, more sustained lines, and dazzling
runs until the climax of a solo, making them integral parts
of a gradually developed musical structure.

Discipline is also a part of *Moritat* (the durable figure

Mack the Knife of course) but here Rollins's approach is a
pattern of contrasts. He is not afraid to alternate a swirling
run of notes with a simple, sometimes wittily staccato phrase
or moan. Harmonically, the performance is relatively simple
and recurrent, but for me this is an aspect of its order, not a
weakness. Its outstanding quality however is Rollins's complete and authoritative relaxation and poise. (Remember
when the fashionable adjectives in describing Sonny Rollins
were "surging," "hard-driving," even "angry"?)

Then *Blue 7*. A masterpiece. Like most masterpieces it is
difficult to describe and discuss; it seems to have a life of its
own, and one never hears it without hearing something wonderfully new in it. Its heritage—beginning with Thelonious
Monk's blues *Misterioso* and going through *Vierd Blues*
which Rollins recorded with Miles Davis on *"Collectors
Items"*—is certainly worth noting, but *Blue 7* also exists entirely on its own.

It opens with a quiet, almost noncommittal walk from
Doug Watkins's bass. Then Rollins enters for the theme—
simple, yet firm and very much committed. And technically
quite intriguing by the way, for it is ambiguous—it might
be in either of two keys or both. Flanagan's entry anchors
the key, and from this point on *Blue 7*'s implicit brilliance
is expertly explored.

Blue 7 is one of those rare improvised performances in
which every part is related to every other part, adding up to
a whole (of nearly eleven minutes) greater than the sum of
those parts, with details so subtle and perfectly in place that
it might take a composer hours to arrive at—yet Rollins
made it all up in a recording studio as he went along. It is
as if Rollins conceived of *Blue 7* as a whole, all at once, although we hear him building it logically, from one phrase
to the next.

The key is, as Max Roach once said, Thelonious Monk's

admonition: Why don't we *use* the melody? Why do we throw it away after the first chorus and just use the chords?

But using the melody involves a lot more than simple decorations and embellishments. Almost everything that Sonny Rollins plays here is ingeniously based on the opening theme of *Blue 7*. But Rollins, like Monk, can get inside a melody, elaborate it logically or reduce it to a tantalizing tissue of notes, an essence, and re-build it once more from that outline—Rollins can even build on his elaborations and interpolations.

But the order and logic on *Blue 7* do not all belong to Rollins. Max Roach's assertive portion is subtly built around a triplet figure and a roll; both of which he states early in his solo. (Anyone interested in further and more technical notes on *Blue 7* can try Gunther Schuller's essay on Rollins in the anthology *Jazz Panorama*.)

Thus for all its subtlety *Blue 7* is the kind of performance that almost anyone grasps immediately. That is, it is the kind of performance to use on the middle-aged uncle who wants to know, "Where's the melody in jazz?" It is also the kind of performance to use in introducing jazz to a complete newcomer. And at the same time it is the kind of performance one might use on the most sophisticated musician to show how excellent jazz improvisation can be. *Blue 7* is a masterpiece. (*1964*)

THE WORLD OF
CECIL TAYLOR

(The LP notated here appeared on Candid LP 8006 and featured Taylor with Dennis Charles and Buell Neidlinger, his first recorded drummer and bassist, plus saxophonist Archie Shepp, on the five compositions discussed here. The LP may be hard to come by in the 1980s; although some Candid LPs reappeared on Barnaby, this one did not.)

Cecil Taylor believes (frankly, even bluntly, believes) that his music speaks for itself and that it should be allowed to. I once sat with him on a discussion panel held by the United Nations Jazz Club (devoted to the somewhat forbidding topic of "the future of jazz") when he remarked as much to the attending audience. After one of his recordings had been played for them Taylor said he would prefer not to discuss it; he hoped the music had said it all. Pressed for further comment, Taylor added that his purpose was to give people pleasure, and he hoped the record did that.

Perhaps Cecil Taylor is right. I am reasonably sure his music will speak directly to receptive ears and receptive feelings. Of course, if a man has already decided how all jazz is supposed to sound, and hence how Taylor is supposed to play, he may have a hipster's problem with Taylor's music. (But then he probably doesn't really *listen* to anybody's music anyway.) In any case, there have been several people ready to talk about Cecil's music in print. When Taylor's first LP appeared, Whitney Balliett wrote in *The New Yorker* that it could have "the same revolutionary impact upon modern jazz as the recordings of Charlie Parker," and called his musical imagination "astonishing." When his second release appeared in 1958, I decided (in *The American Record Guide*) that he was "almost an *avant-garde* by himself. . . . His way may very well be *the* way of the future; it will surely be a part of it." Reviewing more recent releases, Dick Hadlock in *Down Beat* called Taylor's music, "a significant step in a direction that more and more young musicians are turning." Larry Gushee said in *The Jazz Review* of another Taylor LP: "This kind of record compensates for the assembly-line products that so frequently come the way of the jazz reviewer."

Almost all of Taylor's reviews have said that his music makes demands on his listeners—demands for attention and involvement. But, as I say, perhaps Taylor is right, for I expect that the strong and immediate emotional impact of his improvising is self-evident, and for many people it is all the encouragement needed for their close attention—and strong reaction.

If you want to try Taylor's way and go directly to the music, may I suggest you go directly to *This Nearly Was Mine* on this LP. Taylor is giving a popular ditty a strikingly individual improvisational treatment; and I think he is turning it into a blues, so to speak, as authentically the blues as any jazz. I think Cecil Taylor knows some fundamental things about the blues and their meaning. It would be easy for anyone with ears attuned to contemporary concert music to speak knowingly of some of Taylor's "sources." Taylor borrows from outside jazz as well as from within, but jazzmen always have. Like the best jazzmen, he can transform and transmute what he borrows into his own version of the jazz language—and such transformation is a problem that Cecil Taylor is very much aware of. His music seems to me so little a pastiche that to list Taylor's influences—even his jazz influences—becomes perhaps almost irrelevant. Taylor is very personal *and* traditional. A paradox? Yes, and it applies to Louis Armstrong, Lester Young, Duke Ellington, Charlie Parker, Thelonious Monk . . .

Cecil Taylor (to get to the part he wants in these notes) was born in New York City in 1933. He began with private piano teachers, studied at the New York College of Music, and later spent four years at the New England Conservatory. Before forming his own groups, which played his own music, he gigged with such mainstream jazzmen as Hot Lips Page, Lawrence Brown, and Johnny Hodges. With a quartet featuring Steve Lacy's soprano saxophone, Buell Neidlinger's bass, and Dennis Charles's drums, Taylor opened the Five Spot Cafe, Cooper Square, New York. With the same quartet, Taylor played at the 1957 Newport Jazz Festival. His more recent engagements have been with the musicians heard in this recital. For three weeks, they were working both at the Showplace in Greenwich Village and as actor-musicians in the cast of Jack Gelber's long-run play, *The Connection,* at the Living Theatre.

Taylor's new horn companion, Archie Shepp, comes from Philadelphia and is a graduate of Goddard College, where he studied playwriting. Shepp has completed several plays and is not at all sure he would not rather write plays than continue as a professional jazzman. It seems to me that on *Air* and *Lazy Afternoon* he uses what he has absorbed from others (from Sonny Rollins and John Coltrane for two) as the most effective horn companion I have heard in any Cecil Taylor quartet. Why couldn't a man play jazz *and* write plays?

Buell Neidlinger was born in the very charming town of Westport, Connecticut, in 1936. His first instrument was cello, and he constantly threatens to leave jazz for symphony work on bass or cello. In 1960, he was a member of two

Jimmy Giuffre groups which seemed almost permanent fix-
tures at the Five Spot, but he has been a sustaining member
of the Cecil Taylor cadre in almost every one of its manifes-
tations. If I were to slip up again and start talking *about*
this music, I would invite you to hear Neidlinger behind
Taylor on *This Nearly Was Mine,* easily Buell's best thing
on records, I believe.

Dennis Charles has also been a member of each of the
Taylor quartets. He was born in St. Croix in the Virgin
Islands in December 1933. He is a self-taught drummer, but
he readily admits what is readily evident, that Art Blakey is
his favorite musician. Charles also works with calypso and
mambo groups and with some of the Hammond organists
that are a mainstay in the bars along 125th Street in New
York. His more sophisticated jobs have also included the Gil
Evans orchestra. The rapport between Taylor and Charles,
emotional and musical, seems to me exceptional.

The most thorough study of Cecil Taylor's recordings
(reprehensibly thorough, if his music shouldn't be discussed)
was done a couple of years ago by Gunther Schuller, who
called him then the foremost of the small number of jazz
composer-performers whose work spills over into the areas
removed from tonal centers. (Since Schuller wrote in 1958,
there have appeared several other jazzmen who do that, of
course; things move very fast in jazz.) Schuller said that what
Taylor does is however, "quite logical and, in my opinion,
imaginative and stimulating. . . . Throughout his playing
Taylor manages to retain a very close rapport between
the structure of the composition and that of the improvisation . . ." Schuller also said that when Taylor was at his
most adventurous he was never arbitrary but simply letting
the force and logic of a musical idea carry him and that like
Thelonious Monk, Taylor plays passages in which the overall musical shape and direction take precedent over the ac-

tual notes. The choice of notes is secondary to the larger musical contours. In short, what Cecil Taylor does has a musical reason, and not a merely academic one, for being.

Taylor's music is demanding (as I imply above, really listening to any music can be demanding), but the things about which Schuller is speaking are not obscure nor necessarily the esoterica of a trained atonal composer. They are often things that anyone can hear and take pleasure in. For example, on Taylor's *E. B.*, the opening theme itself (which immediately put me in mind of an extension of Parker's *Moose the Mooche* or Rollins's *Oleo*) is, in one form or another, almost constantly either close by or actually in range, sometimes suggested in Taylor's left hand, sometimes elaborated in his right. Or take *Lazy Afternoon:* no matter what happens, the theme is never really abandoned in that performance, and because it is a melody we are all likely to be quite familiar with, it is especially enlightening to follow the various uses Taylor puts it to. To make one more uncalled-for suggestion, I invite you to hear the two-bar exchanges between Taylor and Charles toward the end of *Air*. The two players have soon reversed the usual roles of who answers whom, and Taylor sometimes imitates Charles's drum patterns. (*1961*)

IV
Criticism, Critics, and Scholarship

ॐ

JAZZ, THE PHONOGRAPH, AND SCHOLARSHIP*

My tasks in the Smithsonian Institution's Division of Performing Arts are primarily neither scholarly nor curatorial. The Division is there as a part of the Smithsonian's efforts to be, in the phrase of the Secretary, S. Dillon Ripley, a "museum without walls," and we put performers on stages to do whatever they do before audiences. As Director of the Jazz Program, I produce monthly concerts during the theatrical season. The program leaflets for these concerts carry, in part, the following words:

> It has been said that jazz and its remarkable history have been intrinsically tied to the phonograph record. Through recordings, the musical word spread rapidly, a creative player's innovations could be absorbed quickly. A trumpeter in St. Louis, or an orchestrator in New York, could learn of (and if capable, build on) the contributions of a player from New Orleans almost overnight. At the same time, jazz is a player's art, and however much we might learn from the musical notation of a brilliant improvisation by Charlie Parker, or from studying the score of an Ellington work, we learn vastly more by hearing them played by Parker, or the Ellington orchestra. And if we can no longer hear Parker or Ellington, we can hear their records.

The pioneer writers on jazz in the 1930s recognized that improvisational jazz was uniquely suited to the phonograph,

* This essay, in slightly different form, was originally delivered at a Bicentennial conference "The Phonograph and Our Musical Life" held December 7-10, 1977, at Brooklyn College, City University of New York, the Music Department, organized by H. Wiley Hitchcock.

which could preserve for posterity—in an ultimate twentieth-century American paradox—music which was sometimes made up on the spur of the moment, and which has repeatedly demonstrated, I am convinced, that an impromptu expression may have the skill, the texture, the depth, and the durability of a work of art.

What the pioneering observers did not recognize quite so readily is that the existence of the phonograph has had a direct and identifiable effect on the remarkably rapid and widespread development of the jazz idiom. Indeed, one might say that, above all others, jazz musicians have met the artistic challenge implicit in the existence of the phonograph in terms of both instrumental and stylistic development.

Every musician knows (and every critic should know) that there is no substitute for live performance. Yet it was not necessary for the younger musicians of the 1920s—those to whom the leadership ultimately fell in the 1930s—to have heard Louis Armstrong live in order to have absorbed, used, made personal, or extended his remarkable innovations. Beginning in 1923, they heard him on recordings and learned him from recordings.

The New Orleans trumpeter Henry "Red" Allen, Jr., one of Armstrong's earliest followers, once patiently explained to an interviewer that it was not so much that they both came from the remarkable musical environment of the Crescent City: Allen had absorbed Armstrong's music from recordings—just like everybody else. And Allen, growing up in the days of the wind-up phonograph, had an opportunity not now generally available to younger musicians: he learned the music in all the keys simply by adjusting the old speed screw on the household's Victrola and playing along.

Such stories as Allen's might be repeated endlessly for

every half-decade of the music, including the present one. And suffice it to say that anyone who makes any kind of sustained scholarly or critical statements about jazz and its history and development needs to know the recorded repertory, as much of it as possible and preferably all of it.

Indeed, there are obviously dangers for the scholar in not knowing the recordings and not acknowledging their power. I offer the following vignettes in evidence:

Recently in Washington a black pianist, professionally a maintenance man of the grounds at Howard University, was presented on Sunday morning television. He was there to play blues piano, and he was described as the carrier of an old and durable and important American musical tradition. He certainly was that. But there is one aspect of Afro-American life which many whites, many folklorists, and many jazz critics do not seem to realize—that is, that there is nothing very remarkable about a non-professional black man or woman playing blues piano for his own pleasure and self-enlightenment—nothing more remarkable than the ability of many a middle-aged white housewife to knock off *Humoresque* or Mozart's *Turkish March* as a result of girlhood piano lessons.

But to go back to our Howard bluesman: when he sat down to play, what came out was a reasonably respectable version of Avery Parrish's *After Hours,* a national hit throughout the 1940s for the Erskine Hawkins band and a piece that almost any pianist, amateur or professional, black or white, with an awareness of what was going on at that time tried to learn. It seems to me that any discussion of what that Howard pianist was doing, and what he represented in cultural terms, needs to recognize and deal with the fact that he owes a major debt to the phonograph.

A second vignette. A number of years ago, a prominent American folklorist made a recording field-trip to the rural

South. The results of his tapings were later released on commercial recordings with copious notes which, for the Negro music involved, spoke of the performers as isolated from the main highways and cultural currents, hence carriers of a "pure" and undefiled musical tradition. Blues performances in irregular choruses of twelve and one-half measures followed by eleven measures were seen as evidence of the fact that the blues was once a "spontaneous" and "free" form. Songs about trains inspired annotative passages about the meaning of railroads and travel in Afro-American life and in the blues tradition, etcetera.

Well, it happened that the folkorist had apparently not checked out the recent rhythm-and-blues hits before he undertook his field trip. Indeed, if he was like some folklorists, he probably scorned such music as a commercial corruption of a purer tradition. However, performer after performer on his recordings was clearly trying to imitate records that could be heard and enjoyed in the jukebox down at the crossroads tavern or in someone's record collection or on a local black radio station. In other words, the folklorist had recorded the efforts of amateurs to imitate the professionals they admired. As for the "irregular" blues choruses, they might well have been the result of simple musical inability.

For example, a singer identified as Forest City Joe performed a piece credited to Joe B. Pugh (presumably the singer) titled *Stop Breaking Down*. But Forest City Joe was clearly basing his performance on Sonny Boy Williamson's 1945 recording *Stop Breaking Down,* with Williamson listed as composer. But Williamson's record was in turn based on Robert Johnson's 1937 recording! *Drop Down Mama* performed by one Fred McDowell clearly derived from Sleepy John Estes's 1935 recording of the same title. If I attribute the composer attribution, John Estes, to some research at the record company (Atlantic) which released our folklorist's

McDowell version, I hope the reader may allow me that small bit of cynicism. In any case, Sonny Boy Williamson, Robert Johnson, and Sleepy John Estes, for all their limitations, are superior performers to Forest City Joe or Fred McDowell.

A third vignette: As some of you know, in the 1940s there was an intense revival of interest in New Orleans jazz. On the positive side, it involved some interesting and important discographical, biographical, and critical work. On the negative side, it involved the critical position (which became prevalent in some intellectual circles) that the only authentic jazz, was New Orleans jazz.

Some reputedly neglected but reputedly authentic artists were recorded during this period, and one such was clarinetist George Lewis. When Lewis said that his favorite clarinetist was Artie Shaw, his partisans were somewhat taken aback. But then, one could always retreat to the high ground that the artist is not necessarily the best judge of his own talent. When Lewis recorded a medium-tempo blues titled (by the record's producer) *St. Philip Street Breakdown,* some said that it was now possible for the listener to hear and take pleasure in an authentic, eloquent echo of New Orleans's glorious past. But alas, to anyone aware of the early 1940s' recorded jazz repertory, Lewis was attempting to reproduce some ensemble figures from Woody Herman's *Chips Boogie Woogie* and from Benny Goodman's (and Count Basie's) *Gone With "What" Wind*—and not doing so very well, I am obliged to add. His effort also to use Goodman's *Soft Winds* threw Lewis badly since *Soft Winds* has a substitute chord progression.*

---

* The project known as the National Tune Index, an effort to catalogue all American-composed melodies, is coming upon similar evidence. So far only through pre-Revolutionary music, and thus relying only on printed music, the project reports that it has already discovered that piece after

Somewhat opposite, in praising trombonist Dickie Wells's solo on *Symphonic Scronch* in his excellent book *Jazz: Its Evolution and Essence,* André Hodeir did not know that it was largely based on Charlie Green's solo from Fletcher Henderson's *The Gouge of Armour Avenue.* Hodeir had evidently not heard the Henderson record. Indeed, if he had, he might even have reinforced his praise of Wells, for although Wells largely reproduces Green's notes, the rhythmic nuances of his playing are instructively innovative for the instrument.

One final vignette, and with this one we are more directly in the domain of criticism and education rather than of scholarship. One of the most successful jazz ensembles in the United States is the Preservation Hall Band from New Orleans. The group does not produce hit records, but it does tour our cultural institutions, particularly our college campuses, year after year, and it is billed as an honorable preserver of a great tradition. Now, anyone who knows the music of Sidney Bechet or Jelly Roll Morton or King Oliver's Creole Jazz Band or Jimmy Noone or the early Louis Armstrong groups could not possibly agree with such a billing. Perhaps the average listener cannot discern that most of the Preservation Hall players are spirited amateurs, some of whom do not know their instruments, do not play in tune, and are putting on a show for white folks—who, alas, still view Afro-Americans and their music as exotics. But I do not think that an educator or music historian can allow himself such ignorance. And the answer for him lies in a knowledge of the recording of Morton, Bechet, Oliver, and the rest.   (*1977*)

---

piece, long thought to be anonymous "folk" music, as professionally written and published musical work. The proposition that the United States has a tradition of "folk" music in the European sense seems to be growing daily more dubious.

ॐ

CAUTIONS AND CONGRATULATIONS

An Outsider's Comments on the
Black Contribution to American
Musical Theater*

Some of what I have to say on the subject of musical theater and the black contribution will be personal. I hope it is not so personal as not to be useful.

I will begin with a personal story. When I first moved to the Washington, D.C., area—it was early 1972—I lived in a surburban section which was integrated, mixed, and offered me neighbors whose politics would generally be called liberal. One of the tenets of their view of race relations in this country was that Afro-Americans are "culturally deprived."

I realize that in using such a term they were trying to address a serious and continuing problem. But on the other hand, suppose we look at the question from another point of view, from the point of view of every American's real culture. Here were American liberals, largely white (integration or no), who in their real cultural lives try to sing black, make music black, dance black, move black, and talk black, but calling blacks "culturally deprived." American blacks had, in a single generation produced Leontyne Price, Mahalia Jackson, and Sarah Vaughan, yet they are "culturally deprived." A people who had not only shown

---

* This essay in slightly different form was delivered at a 1984 conference *The Black Contribution to American Musical Theater* jointly sponsored by Morgan State College and the Peabody Institute, and directed by Dominque-Rene de Lerma.

they could absorb and carry European musical culture at the level of André Watts or Shirley Verett, but who could come up with a musical culture as original and compelling as Duke Ellington's. "Culturally deprived" may be the most condescending of all the unconsciously condescending phrases that we have consented to use.

I offer the foregoing, however, partly because what is true of our cultural life in general is also true of our musical theater. Most of the characteristics that we think of as "American" in our musicals are Afro-American. The things that make the great songwriters—Jerome Kern, Irving Berlin, George Gershwin, Cole Porter, Harold Arlen, and the rest—seem American, American and not transplanted Viennese like their predecessors Victor Herbert, Rudolf Friml, and Sigmund Romberg, are (to put it briefly) the syncopations and the blue notes that come from Afro-American music.

The same sort of thing is true of our theatrical dance. Tap dancing is obvious enough: it is an Afro-American transformation of clog dancing. But actually, almost any dancing in which the body moves with the hips loose and flexible, with easy horizontal body movement below the waist, is Afro-influenced. Even the "modern dance" of Isadora Duncan and Martha Graham is admittedly black-influenced, although the influences are subtler and more transmuted than in our other forms of theatrical dance.

I am also convinced that our comic attitudes, our modes of theatrical comedy have been pervasively influenced by the comedy of blacks. But there we are on less firm ground with the influences more difficult to pin down and demonstrate. However, comedy is a subject I shall return to below.

So it seems clear enough that the black influence on our musical theater is pervasive, even fundamental. But what about the accomplishments of blacks themselves in musical theater? Here the story is a bit different.

Take songwriting: Who would be the tunesmiths whose work we would need to consider? At a minimum, Will Marion Cook, Maceo Pinkard, Eubie Blake, James P. Johnson, Fats Waller—plus the man who openly wanted to write a hit Broadway show and never did, Duke Ellington.

Let me single out Eubie Blake from that list. And let me say at the beginning that I have the highest respect for Blake's career and his accomplishments. If we are going to discuss his best songwriting, however, we name *Memories of You* and *I'm Just Wild About Harry* from *Shuffle Along*. We might add only *You're Lucky to Me* from *Shuffle Along*'s sequels, its revivals with new music, and from Blake's other shows. And that is frankly not a very large body of distinguished song-writing. It can't compare with that of such relatively minor Broadway tunesmiths as, say, Jimmy McHugh or Harold Rome.

However, if we look at Blake's full *œuvre*, it would include the really fine early piano pieces like *Charleston Rag, Fizz Water, Chevy Chase*, and the picture of his total accomplishments alters.

The same would be true of James P. Johnson, with only *Old Fashioned Love* and *Charleston* in his folio of memorable songs, but with over half a dozen outstanding piano works from *Carolina Shout* through *Caprice Rag* and *Jingles* to *Mule Walk*.* And true of Waller: he had perhaps one or two more memorable show tunes—*Ain't Misbehavin'* and

---

* Johnson's career in musical theater would make an interesting subject for study, from *Runnin' Wild* and *Messin' Around* in the 1920s through *Sugar Hill* in 1931. An unperformed opera, *De Organizer*, with a libretto by Langston Hughes, survives among Johnson's manuscripts in the possession of his family.

Black and Blue are outstanding, *Willow Tree* and *Lonesome Me* exceptional. But with Waller the list of distinguished theater songs again runs out quickly and one turns to such keyboard works as *A Handful of Keys, Valentine Stomp* and his recorded piano interpretations of the works of others (*I Ain't Got Nobody, Tea for Two,* etc.) to gain a fairer picture of his stature.

Ellington, as I say, is another matter. But for all his many distinguished songs, he never composed for a successful show. And his real work was his instrumental compositions for his orchestra, work which, for some of us, earned him the title of our greatest composer, regardless of musical category or style.*

On dance: If one makes a list of the great black theatrical dancers—Bill Robinson through Honi Coles, John Bubbles and the Nicholas Brothers through Baby Lawrence—one realizes that their dancing does not go beyond the "specialty" dance or its more opulent counterpart, the "production number." They did not transform their work into the kind of dance-drama we see in the self-choreographed work of Fred Astaire and Gene Kelly—the dance integrated into plot and character development, the dance expressing dramatic relationships and conflicts—nor did they seem particularly interested in doing so. This, despite the presence of such distinguished (but Caribbean-oriented) dance choreographers as Katherine Dunham and Pearl Primus.

My further thoughts on dance might best be put in the form of some questions: Whose work is truly "blacker," Alvin Ailey or Jerome Robbins? Ailey or Twyla Tharpe? Ailey or Bob Fosse?

---

* However, Ellington's considerable work in musical theater, like the rest of his musical biography, is well known in general, but unexplored in detail. For two examples, the 1966 musical *Pousse Café* failed and went unrecorded; and an opera, *Queenie Pie,* one of his last projects, remains to be produced.

Of course, I do not mean to imply by these more or less rhetorical questions that Ailey should be "blacker" in his designs or movements. He and the Dance Theater of Harlem are fully entitled to undertake any kind of dancing they wish to and entitled to full praise as they succeed at it. But I cannot help wishing that a master choreographer would come along and use that heritage of breathtaking grace and originality that John Bubbles and the Nicholas Brothers, the classic Lindyhoppers and the latest break dancers have provided, and produce a major Afro-American story-telling dance.*

On comedy: One of the most difficult and touchy subjects in all our culture is Negro-American comedy, its past, its present, and its influence on us all. I will put my first thoughts in the form of some questions and some suggestions for thought, research, and criticism: Is there a right way, a wise and fair way, to understand the celebrated talents of Bert Williams and Miller and Lyles, a way to hear their many surviving recordings with full appreciation?

If we compare the traditional comic, saucy servants with Jack Benny's Rochester (Eddie Anderson) might we not better understand Rochester's apparently subservient character and attitudes? Are not he, and many another comic black servant in our dramatic past, contemporary American expressions of a comic tradition that is as old as the Greeks and Romans? And as meaningful as are Molière's several "Nicoles"? And aren't they best understood and evaluated in that way?

Does King Lear's "wise fool" perhaps tell us something

---

* To pursue my fantasy further, if Michael Jackson has the potential as a dancer he seems to have, and were willing to work at it, perhaps Geoffrey Holder might create for him a drama-dance both intimate and grandiose. Then we might have a choreographer and dancer who could do for Afro-American dance what Ellington did for Afro-American music.

about Steppin Fetchit? That is, is it possible that in his de-
tached way, Fetchit expressed insights and concerns that the
whites who surrounded him did not have?

What might we learn if we juxaposed Moms Mabley and
Minnie Pearl? Might we decide that, after all, they were
really quite close together, perhaps that they had much the
same act?

I have heard it said that Burns and Allen were heavily
influenced by the black vaudeville team Butterbeans and
Susie. Is that true? And if it is, what is the nature of that
and similar black-white influences? (It would have to go
deeper than lines and jokes of course.)

What was the real meaning of blackface? Was it entirely
a matter of making facile jokes at the expense of black people? Or, as Robert C. Toll suggests in *Blacking Up,* did
putting on the theatrical mask of blackness enable any performer to make sometimes shrewd comments on the events,
attitudes, and mores of the times which he could not make
otherwise so effectively?

Finally, is a truly demeaning blackface really dead? We
may no longer use the make-up, but for a generation that
makes celebrities out of, let us say, Mick Jagger and Janis
Joplin can one say that a symbolic blackface is dead? And
what is the real meaning of its survival?

By way of further comment, I would like to paraphrase
some thoughts which I have prepared as annotations for the
Smithsonian's proposed record albums reconstructing *Shuffle Along* and *Runnin' Wild* from surviving archival recordings of their songs and comedy by cast members.

A WORD ABOUT MILLER AND LYLES

Undoubtedly many of us will be surprised—even shocked—
on hearing the comedy sketches of Miller and Lyles for the
first time. And that is probably a good thing. But it is also
a thing worth thinking about.

Many of us are more used to hearing comparable material performed by whites in blackface by the likes of Moran and Mack ("The Two Black Crows"), Amos 'n' Andy (for whom Miller and Lyles later actually wrote material), Pick and Pat (Molasses 'n' January), and the rest. And done by performers who are not black, such comedy necessarily seems demeaning to most of us today.

But what if it is written by blacks and performed by them?

Perhaps the nature of the audience is also a part of the picture. A 1920s' Negro audience might have taken Miller and Lyles material as a keenly observed and legitimate satire on the pomposity or the foolishness of certain of their fellows. And in fact, Miller and Lyles, as comedian-authors, were not merely repeating clichés of the minstrel stage; they drew up their types and their sketches also from personal observation and first-hand experience.

Somehow white audiences have traditionally seemed all too ready to take such material, not as works of a comic imagination, but as a literal portrayal of all Negro Americans. And many liberals, black and white, have accordingly been quick to condemn such comedy out-of-hand. And that indeed makes for a baffling dilemma in American life.

We did not take the adroit fumblings of Gracie Allen as insulting to anyone. Nor do we call the crude buffooneries of the Three Stooges insulting to whites. We did not take the agonized tribulations of the Goldbergs as a point-of-departure for anti-Semitism. Nor was Fibber McGee received as a generalization about dumb Irishmen.

But somehow white audiences have most often taken Negro American comedy—even if legitimately observed by blacks—as a tissue of literal realities and worthy generalizations. Whites somehow cannot seem to respond that here is a man behaving like a fool (even behaving like the "wise fool" of comedic tradition), as some men do and I might do, but rather that here is a black fool—and what else should one expect?

The dilemma continues. Unquestionably, the largely white audiences who attended *Ain't Misbehavin'* on Broadway in the 1970s take the good-spirited, Fats Waller-inspired clowning of that show differently than a Negro audience would—or than a Negro audience would have taken the real Fats Waller in 1938. And one wonders if the sometimes superb scatology of certain contemporary black comics is not a part of an acute and subtle defense mechanism against the near-impossibility that a black comedian play the clown or fool—as any comedian must—while never seeming to insult his fellow blacks on the one hand, nor to cater to the middle-class proprieties on the other. (In that sense, Miller and Lyles may have had a freedom not available to Redd Foxx, Richard Pryor, and Eddie Murphy.)

In any case, there might be much for us to learn if we could approach Miller and Lyles at the level of their intentions. And then ask if Miller and Lyles actually succeeded at benignly satirical comment on the kind of pomposity, pretentiousness, and foolishness that tempts most of us, and conquers some of us. At least then we might be able to give them their due as comic performers of skill, shrewdness, and insight, and as artists of great influence on tones and the attitudes that are now found in American comedy of all kinds. We might also discover somethings about ourselves as well.

For final comment and guidance, I would like to turn to Duke Ellington. In 1938 he was asked to contribute to the first issue of a new publication, the *Negro Actor* (the issue of July 15 to be exact). From his hospital room, where he was recovering from minor surgery, he sent the following:

The sky-line from my windows in the Wickersham hospital is an inspiring sight. I have spent three weeks in bed here, not too ill to be thrilled daily by a view of these skyscrapers, and with plenty of time for ample meditation.

It is natural, perhaps, that I should think of many subjects, some serious, some fanciful. I spent some time comparing the marvelous sky-line to our race, likening the Chrysler tower, the Empire State building and other lofty structures to the lives of Bert Williams, Florence Mills and other immortals of the entertainment field.

I mused over the qualities which these stars possessed that enabled them to tower as far above their fellow artists as do these buildings above the sky-line.

And it seemed to me, from where I was lying, that in addition to their great talent, the qualities which have made really great stars are those of simplicity, sincerity, and a rigid adherence to the traditions of our own people.

We are children of the sun and our race has a definite tradition of beauty and glory and vitality that is as rich and powerful as the sun itself. These traditions are ours to express, and will enrich our careers in proportion to the sincerity and faithfulness with which we interpret them.

ဦ

HOMAGE À HODEIR*

To come directly to the point, it seems to me that André Hodeir's *Jazz: Its Evolution and Essence* survives its first twenty-four years as one of the most compelling books ever written on the music. And I have no doubt that it will survive twenty-four more—and many more beyond that.

It was certainly a book for its own time. To anyone who did not live through it (and, by now, even to those of us who did) the controversy caused by the innovations of Charlie Parker and his associates may seem a puzzling phenomenon.

* Introduction to the updated Grove Press Black Cat edition of André Hodeir's *Jazz: Its Evolution and Essence.*

Parker's music was even declared to be not jazz at all by one pioneering and influential French commentator. And as a part of the picture, certain American observers and fans retreated to a position that little or nothing of merit had happened in the music since the maturity of the New Orleans style. On the other hand, there were younger enthusiasts for whom jazz started with Charlie Parker and whatever had preceded him was worth scant attention, or perhaps none at all.

Yet here was a critic not only willing to champion Parker's legitimacy but to give us his thoughtful reasons on the matter; willing, indeed, and able to raise and discuss some fundamental questions about the music and its tradition, its soloists, its composers, and its development.

Here was a critic who not only could enlighten us about Parker but who had some highly important things to say about Louis Armstrong and his pivotal position in the history of jazz. And who could give us crucial insight into the accomplishments and the genius of Ellington.

In effect, then, André Hodeir's book was a peace-making effort which in the long run has succeeded superbly, a book which has now persuaded two generations of listeners and critics to see the music whole.

And by writing a truly excellent book for its own time, Hodeir demonstrated that excellence, as always, survives its time and assumes a permanent place in our lives.

Some early reactions to *Jazz: Its Evolution and Essence* were interesting. Those fans who already liked Parker generally welcomed the book, although I suspect that fewer of them read and absorbed it.

Some early reviewers said, in effect, that they could not understand how, in an aesthetic field, modernists could be declared to be "better" than the tradition. But of course André Hodeir did not say that Charlie Parker was "better"

than Louis Armstrong. He did say that he found Parker a
better improvisor than Mezz Mezzrow and he gave us his
reasons.

Other reviewers (and some musicians) found André Hodeir's comments occasionally rarified and wanting in an intimate knowledge of the milieu in which the music was produced and of the attitudes of the musicians who produced it.

That was a complaint which Hodeir sought to rectify in
subsequent stays in the United States. But surely one answer
is that Dickie Wells's *Taxi War Dance* solo or Louis Armstrong's on *Big Butter and Egg Man* or Miles Davis's on
Move are remarkable musical experiences no matter under
what circumstances they were produced. And it is their remarkable qualities, which concerned Hodeir, that should
lead us to the day-to-day lives of the men who produced
them, and not the other way around.

Finally, there were the fundamentalist comments which
held one way or another that jazz would remain alive so
long as people responded with their feet and not with their
heads.

I do not quite know how André Hodeir feels about dancing or foot-patting; he does not tell us. But surely the point
is that those listeners who are responding *only* with their
feet may be missing whole areas of musical pleasure and en-
lightenment. (And what if jazz attracted *musicians* capable
only of responding to the feet—or, as Lester Young once put
it, only with their bellies?)

My praise of this book could not be totally unqualified of
course. I prefer the original French title of the volume—in
translation, *Men and Problems of Jazz*. It may be clumsy
English but it is a straightforward yet cautious description
of the book's intentions. I do not believe that M. Hodeir
quite succeeded in defining the term *swing* for us. Nor does
it seem to me just to date all artistry in jazz as beginning

with Louis Armstrong. And M. Hodeir can be a severe critic at moments when severity may not be the most persuasive attitude.

But enough. It is not a critic's business to impose his opinions on us, but to help us (sometimes force us) to clarify our own.

To say that André Hodeir is one of the few real critics to have written on jazz is not to do him justice. In this book, he proved himself to be the kind of critic that the observers of any artistic pursuit should be pleased to have encountered—indeed, the caliber of critic that perhaps only a truly artistic pursuit could have attracted.   (*1979*)

(If I have anything to add to the above, five years later, it would be not so much about M. Hodeir, as about criticism. And about the fact that the ultimate basis for any critical judgment is feeling. No matter how well a critic has brought all his knowledge to bear, no matter how well he has listened and absorbed, how justly he has compared the music at hand with all that has gone before it, no matter how well he has given us the *why* and the *how* of his judgments, at the final moment of judgment he has only feeling to fall back on. And as I say, his feelings are his own.

(A critic says, in effect, this music is good for mankind, or not good, and therefore he sets his own feelings before mankind. It is a presumptuous and, indeed, dangerous thing to do. The critic, like the creative artist, exposes his innermost feelings, naked and vulnerable, before the world and presumes to suggest to the world that it should care about those feelings and make them its own.

(Perhaps therefore the critic and the artist have more in common than some artists would care to admit. In any case, each man's task takes a courage and a fortitude that the other might contemplate—and that their audiences might contemplate as well.)

CULTURAL DIGGINGS

Look out: I have the feeling that before this is over I'm going to be recommending some scholarly research. But meanwhile, bear with me because I think you'll enjoy the ride.*

Take this phrase:

Probably nobody knows how old that one is, and it may be that nobody still living knows where it originally came from. In the twenties it was known as (among other things) *Mecca Flat Blues* (after a South Side Chicago apartment house) and as *Nobody Knows the Way I Feel This Morning.*

The earliest published version of it I know is as one of two strains in a Jelly Roll Morton blues that he sometimes called *Tom Cat Blues* and other times called *Midnight Mama.* (That's the version given above.)

Sidney Bechet made a beautiful record of it in 1940 under the *Nobody Knows* title. At about the same time, it was used as the basis of a ridiculous pop ditty (deliberately ridiculous) that Ella Fitzgerald recorded, called (are you ready?) *I Want the Waiter with the Water.* A more recent use of it was in John Lewis's score for an Italian movie called *A Milanese Story,* and it is currently played by the MJQ in the piece called *In a Crowd.*

But my brief account of the recorded history of the phrase

* Notation approximate in musical examples.

241

probably doesn't scratch the surface of its use as a basis for
written themes, nor its use as an interpolation, in hundreds
of variants and permutations, by soloists as they improvise.

It is one of those phrases that just seem to have been indigenous parts of Afro-American musical lore from the beginning, as it were, and whose meaning for each successive
generation of players has been tenacious.

There are many, many such phrases. Take this one (I'll
give it in a very early style):

Now, nearly everybody, even some younger players, calls
that one *Funky Butt*. The old-timers in New Orleans say it
was *Buddy Bolden's Blues* or, played faster, *Bolden's Stomp*.
According to Rudi Blesh's *They All Played Ragtime*, it was
commonplace along the Mississippi among dockworkers and
boatmen long before Bolden, well back into slavery times,
as the basis of a bawdy ditty even then called *Funky Butt*.

It found its way into a ragtime piece called *St. Louis
Tickle* in 1904 (my reason for the 2/4 time signature above).
Many players were fond of it during the 1930s. Try Lionel
Hampton's intro to his Victor recording of *Dinah*. Or try
the allusion to it that guitarist Irving Ashby makes on the
Hampton Victor record called *Open House*. (Ashby also
echos, by the way, one of Louis Armstrong's vocal breaks
from *Hotter Than That* in that intro.) And try Charlie
Christian's intro to *Gone With What Draft* or *Gilly*.

Art Tatum used the "funky butt" motive to form a fine
(and surely wry) ending to several of his versions of *Indiana*. More recently, I heard Clark Terry allude to it, asked

him about it, and discovered that he still calls it "funky butt."

Then there's this one:

It has been called *The Snags* or *Snag 'Em*. The title comes from *Sam Jones Has Done Snagged His Britches* which (I'm guessing) is probably the name of an old ministrel song that used the phrase.

In the 1920s, it was all over the place—as a plaintive tuba chorus on Ollie Powers's *Play That Thing*, as the theme of *Snag 'Em Blues*. In a different version, it is also one of the traditional themes that James P. Johnson used in his extended *Yamekraw* rhapsody, a piece which is a treasure-trove of the sort of phrases I'm discussing here.

In King Oliver's slow *Snag It* the phrase was considerably transmuted into this antiphonal riff:

And Jimmy Yancey used the "snag 'em" lick as one of the breaks in his fine *Yancey's Bugle Call*.

I am told that the late Dan Burley, once managing editor of the Harlem *Amsterdam News*, knew dozens of boogie-woogie and blues bass figures, and had traced them to their historical and regional origins in the South and Southwest. I dearly hope his knowledge was preserved. I think similar

research ought to be done on traditional melodic phrases of
the kind I have been dealing with here. On their origins,
and on the meanings that successive generations have found
in them and the different uses they have put them to. The
results would surely prove to be cultural history of a most
enlightening sort.

So it would seem that certain traditional, indigenous
phrases recur in piece after piece, solo after solo, and seem,
by their very persistence, to have an important cultural
meaning.

However, some phrases don't stay the same. Here is how
one phrase has been modified and developed.

Take this riff:

The phrase seems familiar enough, once one sees it, or
hears it, but I can't cite any early instance of its clear use as
an ensemble or background riff. There is Lionel Hampton's
1945 *Hey-Ba-BaRe-Bop,* but that gets me a bit ahead of my
story.

I do know that Coleman Hawkins used the riff as the basis
of his solo on the 1941 Metronome All Stars recording of
One O'Clock Jump—and such a straightforwardly riffing
solo was rather uncharacteristic for Hawkins. A bit later,
by the way that Hawkins solo was scored for the whole
Count Basie band, and recorded as *Feedin' the Bean,* with
Hawkins sitting in as guest soloist.

In March of 1941, however, the Benny Goodman Sextet
recorded a piece that was at first called *Good Enough To*

Keep, and later retitled *Air Mail Special*. It featured a background riff to Georgie Auld's sax solo that went this way:

Quite an attractive riff, that. I'm personally convinced it came from guitarist Charlie Christian, who was of course, a member of the Goodman group at the time and was later credited as a co-author of the piece. In any case, the two-bar riff is quite characteristic of him.

But notice that what Christian has done is to elaborate, quite ingeniously too, the one-bar riff we started with. And not simply by tacking something on its end, or its beginning, but by an organic fore-and-aft elaboration. It is as if he got at the riff's essence and saw implications no one else had noticed. (I know it sounds a little highfalutin' to put it that way, but that's what he did.)

This same riff, by the way, shows up in the final ensemble choruses of the Basie's band's second (January 1942) recording of *One O'Clock Jump*.

But the matter didn't rest there.

Do you know a little song-form piece from the mid-1950s written by Horace Silver for the Art Blakey Jazz Messengers called *Hippy?* If you do, you're already onto what I'm about to say, because that Charlie Christian *Air Mail Special* riff forms the opening phrase of Silver's eight-bar bop-style melody!

Now, would anybody care to join me in digging around in the records, say, of Don Cherry or Gary Bartz for some version of the phrase?

This is not directly related to the above, but in 1943, Lester Young made a record of *Sometimes I'm Happy* in which, in his last four bars, he interpolated a lovely phrase that all kinds of people picked up on. Singers used it—some still do—when they did the piece (two examples: Dinah Washington, Carmen McRae). Along came Gerry Mulligan and made a piece out of the phrase, *Jeru,* which he recorded with Miles Davis in 1949.

Bud Powell retaliated with his record *So Sorry Please,* based on Prez's phrase and, it would seem, Mulligan's piece too. (Powell gave it a nice title under the circumstances, no?)

The other day I was listening to Columbia's second volume in its complete Bessie Smith series, and I was caught short by the until then familiar title *My Sweetie Went Away (And He Didn't Say Where, When or Why),* a pop tune from 1923. For there is the ultimate origin of the phrase that Lester Young interpolated and elaborated so beautifully, and everybody picked up on.

Black Studies anyone?   (*1971*)

INDEX